Super-Aging Secrets

Angelo V Moca

ISBN-13: 9798771845265

Editor: Haley Paskalides

Printed in the United States of America

Table of Contents

INTRODUCTION

Super-Aging Secrets Revealed

- How to regulate or reduce aging changes.
- How to lessen aging declines rather than treat early disease.
- How survivors, escapers, and extenders live long, active lives.
- Why do some people defy aging while others decline precipitously?
- Is intense activity good, bad, or doesn't matter?
- What do long-lived individuals do to maintain their lifestyles longer?

Has the world been seduced into thinking that medical advancements will somehow save them from chronic disease and injury? Is there any doubt that fountain of youth enthusiasts believe that some new pill, treatment, food, supplement, or other magical discovery is miraculously going to preserve their ability to lead a more prolonged disease and disability-free life? Are we chasing that age-old dream of immortality while suffering from a gradual deterioration of our current standard of living? What's true?

Super-Aging Secrets introduces an educational aging with dignity book focused on the quality of life versus the length of life. We believe that a long-life span is extremely precarious without an associated and parallel health span. In today's high-tech world, seniors have realized that their biggest fear is not death; it's becoming disabled and not being able to take care of themselves.

Curiously, there's a population of people out there known as Super-Agers that live relatively disease and disability-free lives well into their 80's, 90's, and even 100's. And best of all, they don't have any significant chronic problems throughout life. How do they do it?

Is it because they inherited their parent's genes? Are they just lucky? Or do they have common traits and habits? In this book, you'll find out what specific attributes long-lived individuals possess and why they can maintain similar cognitive and physical capacities comparable to people decades younger than them.

Remember, these super-seniors are 80+ years old compared to 40+ middle-aged individuals.

This book is a compendium of aging insights and facts that most people don't know, or what they do know is speculative and general information. Some people are guided or misguided by media sources, and others are not concerned enough to explore the objective truths. Here are a few samples.

- In the study named, It's Never Too Late, fifty men and women of an average age of eighty-seven worked out for ten weeks, increased muscle strength by about 113%, and boosted their walking speed significantly.
- Older people who joined a group activity were in better health, used less medication, had fewer falls, were less lonely, and had a better outlook on life.
- The paradox of aging states that as we grow older, we grow happier. Also, perceived health improves in people with positive attitudes even though objective health declines. In contrast, people with negative views of aging die earlier.
- People who are open to new experiences and have higher levels of learning tend to live longer.
- Exercise is a critical component in preventing mental decline lowering the risk of depression and other mental health challenges.
- Spending less time sitting might increase your lifespan.

These examples are just a few of the dozens of documented aging theories introduced in this book to help reduce aging problems and control associated issues.

This manuscript also introduces a paradigm for living that teaches ways to maintain your standard of living through disciplined and controlled behavior. Maintaining an active lifestyle for life is one of the main focuses of this book.

There are many decisions made throughout life, and in many cases, options and choices are left to your discretion. Educating yourself on aging acumen provides the information necessary to make confident and well-informed choices. Our mission is to provide valid information on leading a healthy, active, and rewarding life FOR LIFE. Find out what it takes to become a Super-Ager!

CHAPTER 1: Super-Aging Secrets "How Old Are You" Evaluation

This chapter will answer a critical question. How do you know if you're aging? If you believe you are, what can you do about it? The "How Old Are You" test is designed to recognize aging deficits before they progress. This evaluation explores typical aging declines and then determines how, or if, aging has affected you. After taking the test, you should decipher whether you have aging issues. You should also recognize that there are things that you could do in your early years that you can't do now. Your next question should then be, "So what CAN I do about it?" The answer to this question is comprehensively covered throughout the book.

What is Aging, and How Is It Defined?

Here Are Some Mainstream Definitions:

Aging is:

1. The Passage of time. The process of becoming older
2. The average point in peoples lives where breakdown exceeds buildup
3. A collection of changes that render us more likely to die
4. The occurrence of physical, psychological, and social change. Some dimensions of aging grow and expand over time, while others decline
5. Aging is the gradual and progressive decline of vital tissues, physical skills, essential capacities, and associated functions (This is our preferred definition that will be referred to throughout this book).

The "How Old Are You Test" was designed to help people identify physical deficits, lost capacities, sense order dysfunctions, and vital tissue changes that have developed over time, resulting in compromised living. These deficits and lost skills are our virtual definition of aging.

Super-Aging Secrets is all about identifying aging problems so that you can deal with them before they worsen or compound into severe issues. You can't deal with aging losses if we don't know what they are. Regretfully, most people don't realize they have a problem until they have incurred a severe physical issue (too late). Let's refer to the football analogy, "Bend but don't break defense." You can recover from the small yardage gains, but you're likely to lose the football game if you give up too many big plays. In life, when significant problems arise, they threaten your long-term vitality, but with minor issues, your ability to rebound and stay healthy is much more likely. If you manage slight losses, you control aging and, in turn, "stay in the game."

This test will help you determine:

1. How old are you physically?
2. Are you aging normally?
3. Are there any skills you could do in the past and can't do now?
4. Do you have any muscle, nerve, swelling, or associated pain issues?

After taking this test, you should assess your aging status. Evaluating what physical skills you're losing or have lost allows you to either:

- Rehabilitate those problems or
- Get treatment if necessary

Take the "How Old Are You" Test

✓ There are 20 questions asked.

Grade yourself, as best you can, a score of 1-5 on each question

1. Severe problems.
2. Major problems
3. Mild problems
4. Minimal problems
5. No problems.

✓ This test is subjective, so you are on your honor. Try to be honest and realistic.

✓ We provide an answer sheet to grade yourself at the end of the chapter.

*All age groups are invited to participate, but we primarily target the middle-aged (40-64) and the aged (65+).

*Remember: This test does not evaluate, or in any way try to access, your "total" length of life. Many people lead a sedate and inactive long life, and this test assesses active and independent lifespan! Big difference.

This test is not conclusive. Even if you're in poor physical condition, you can almost always restore or at least improve your living skills, especially A.D.L.s (Activities of Daily Living).

Evaluation Questions

1. Do you have any problems walking normally without fatiguing, without pain, without a significant limp, all day, as necessary?
2. Do you have any significant range of motion loss in any joint or joints? Maybe there are multiple joints or simply tight and restricted movement overall?
3. Do you have any significant weakness or noticeable strength decline in any muscle or joint in your body? Can you feel changes in many separate areas or total body deficits?
4. Do you have long-term atrophy or muscle wasting anywhere in your body? One area, two or more spots, or total body tissue losses?
5. Are you experiencing any chronic swelling in any area or joint for three months or more? Multiple joints, ankle(s), foot, or feet?
6. Do you have daily stiffness, cramping, or aches and pains that keep you from doing your daily tasks? How often? Occasionally, weekly, or even daily?
7. Can you get up from a deep-seated chair or a lying-down position without pushing off with your hands? Is it easy, hard, in between, or impossible? Is it painful? Any chronic numbness or tingling in any part of the body for three months or more? Maybe multiple areas? Does it radiate to other places?
8. Are you experiencing any significant memory gaps, misplace objects, or do you experience apathy, confusion, or disorientation? Are you getting lost?
9. Have you had major surgery(s), or have you been told you need major surgery? Multiple surgeries often result in numerous associated aging issues. Grade yourself on whether you have fully recovered from these issues/surgeries or now have growing problems.

10. Do you have any gross postural changes or curvatures? Include spine, trunk, arms, hips, pelvic, legs, and feet. Look at yourself in a mirror and look to see if a body part is higher or lower, in or out. While lying on your back, do all body parts touch the ground.

11. Are you being treated for any chronic issues or diseases? One, two, three, or more?

12. Are you using medication(s) for three months or more on a routine basis? One, two, three, or more, over counter or prescription drugs?

13. Do you have any problems dressing, grooming, or doing other everyday tasks? Are you completely independent, or do you need assistance with any daily chores?

14. Do you have balance or equilibrium problems? Do you get dizzy when getting up from a reclined position? Are you unstable, or do you intermittently trip or fall?

15. Have you stopped participating in any activity or sport because of injury or disease for a season, for a year, or made you just quit altogether?

16. Have you been bedridden or non-weight-bearing for long periods? Once for a week or two? Four to eight weeks? Many months? Has it occurred multiple times?

17. Have you been diagnosed or treated for any sense organ or gum disease? Dental, hearing, vision, touch, taste, or smell? Examples: Periodontics, Presbycusis, Presbyopia, Cataracts, Glaucoma, Smell-Taste Disorder, or Touch Sensation Problems.

18. Do you have a sleep disorder such as insomnia, apnea, restless leg disorder, or other sleeping issues? Are you usually sleeping 7-9 hours nightly?

19. Have you experienced any incidental bone fracture(s)?

20. Are you very lean with poor muscle tone? Or are you overweight with high central (belly/hip) fat?

Answer Sheet: 5. No issue, 4. Mild, 3. Moderate, 2. Major, 1. Severe

Question: 1___ 2___ 3___ 4___ 5___ 6___ 7___ 8___ 9___ 10___ = ___

11___ 12___ 13___ 14___ 15___ 16___ 17___ 18___ 19___ 20___ = ___ Total

How did you do?

<u>Seniors: 65 and above:</u>

- 90 plus = Ageless Wonder
- 80-89 = Above Average
- 70-79 = Normal Aging
- 55-69 = Concerning
- Below 55 = Worrisome

<u>Middle-Aged: 40-65:</u>

- 95 plus = Excellent
- 85-94 = Good
- 75-84 = Fair
- 60-74 = Poor
- Below 60 = Distressing

This test was put together to introduce the concept of normal aging vs. Super-Aging. Most people constantly compare aging, how and when it occurs, and the warning signs. By knowing what aging factors to look for, common issues can be addressed and reduced before becoming chronic.

There are a host of questions on the test asking about daily tasks. What could you have done in your earlier years, in contrast to what can you do now, later in life? Have you noticed any functional deteriorations over time? Sadly, aging affects every system in the body over time. These gradual losses increase the risk of acute injuries and diseases that accelerate aging. These losses add up and result in a more flawed lifestyle. Super-Aging's philosophy works to reduce deficits in vital function, which helps maintain the ability to stay active and independent for life.

Aging is directly related to loss of muscle strength, endurance, bone, flexibility, increased body fat, poor balance, and decreased cardio-vascular efficiency. Many other body organ issues are pervasive, including sensory vision, hearing, dental, touch, taste, and smell dysfunctions. Controlling those losses decreases disease and injury incidence, enabling a more prosperous and rewarding lifestyle.

Poor gait, loss of motion, chronic pain, strength deficits, inflammation, sleeping issues, neurological sensation problems, postural curvatures, multi-medication use, major surgeries, and the inability to do routine daily activities directly correlate to cumulative aging deficits. If you can control your deficiencies, you can, in turn, increase your ability to stay healthy and active.

Maintaining a "normal" active lifestyle for life is one of the main takeaways of this book. It's vital to preserve the developmental skills because getting them back becomes increasingly difficult as you age if you lose your daily movement skills. Super-Aging is all about protecting essential functions and abilities.

Of course, some medical treatment is necessary for everyone, but regretfully, too much treatment often results in lifestyle changes. Successful healing can be an oxymoron, and the healing process invariably results in secondary issues and scarring that can never be considered normal. Multiple problems typically occur because scar tissue lacks elasticity, restricts movement, results in adhesions, and frequently causes weakness and pain.

Every time an everyday task or skill is degraded or lost, a little bit of the ability to live an everyday lifestyle is also lost. Slowly, little by little, step by step, life changes for the worse. The more you deteriorate, the more physical skills you lose, the older you become. Remember, this decay process is frequently reversible, and quality of life can change quickly and sometimes permanently if not addressed.

What kind of life do you want? Hopefully, a healthy, active, and independent one. Being old can be a blessing for many but can also curse others. Be careful when others say you're too old to keep doing your regular active routine. They may mean well, or maybe even trying to protect you, but beware, stopping activity also has negative consequences! Living out your later years should not mean restricting your meaningful pastimes. Adjustments may be necessary, but Super-Agers adapt rather than quit. Some eventual care may be required, but the goal is to restore skills instead of compromising your way of life.

This quote from former Notre Dame coach Lou Holtz exemplifies this idea well, "Don't keep me alive by keeping me from living."

CHAPTER 2: Aging Principles

Oscar Wilde once wrote: "The old believe everything, the middle-aged suspect everything, the young know everything." This quote does not criticize generational mentalities but simply observes that perception may not be reality.

Whether you fall into any of these three categories, how we age is unknown, hotly debated, and a conversation starter in virtually every age group. That's what makes these discussions so captivating and thought-provoking.

If you're looking or feeling good, people may ask, what did you do to achieve that? If you're looking or feeling bad, the question becomes; what caused your problems? Regardless of the circumstances, everyone wants to know your secret, or conversely, your predicament.

This book serves to educate all age groups about the pursuit of aging gracefully through flourishing, vigorous living practices. Our primary focus will be on the aging population, starting with the 40+ age group.

Suppression of Premature Aging Issues Is a Lifetime Proposition

We will briefly include the younger generation in this discussion. Young adults must understand that healthy foundations start in the early formative years. Parents are aware that most kids and adolescents (a) won't listen to them and (b) think they already know everything!

Most young adults have an "anything-goes" mentality regarding lifestyle decisions. Having parents that are good role models and who lead by example is a great starter. However, too many young people still live by "what feels right at the time mentality." It's still imperative that parents and teachers make a concerted effort to inform young people that poor lifestyle choices will undoubtedly follow them through their young lives and into their foreseeable future.

Along with other first-world countries, the U.S.A. produces the most unfit, unhealthy, and obese children in modern history. Young adults need to understand that habits established in the early years are harbingers for things to come. Obese and inactive children predominantly become obese and inactive adults. Development of bone and muscle in early life has a protective value in later years.

Our schools have done a poor job educating our children about healthy living. We are currently seeing the increase of early-onset diseases in our youth that were previously only seen in older adult populations. Remodeling health and physical education classes should be a priority for upcoming generations, and more emphasis needs to be on educating adolescents on health and fitness components. Teachers should also introduce a beginning level of applied anatomy and physiology. It would be beneficial if students learned more about body motions or mechanics and less about team sports.

When Do Visible Signs of Aging Begin?

Like other aging components, when and why aging starts are up for debate. Aging can begin anywhere from the late twenties to the early thirties. This book discusses maturity concepts that become apparent in the fifth decade (40+).

Aging beliefs say that this intermediate group (40-60) is suspicious of everything, and they don't know who to trust or what to expect. Regarding medical issues, their intuition is correct because this group will experience numerous unexpected medical problems; that's a virtual assurance. This book will provide tips on how to be prepared.

Middle-aged individuals have the highest incidence of acute and developmental orthopedic problems. Chronic and degenerative conditions can quickly become threatening diseases. How these incidents are handled will most likely determine the ability to stay physically active in later years. A mobile and involved future depends on good decisions during middle age.

Retirement Ages: How to Implement an Ongoing Plan

The older age group (60+) are said to believe everything. Well, here's something these sexagenarians need to believe; if they don't continue to take care of themselves, they're much more likely to have significant issues. Percolating early disability and premature death occurs at accelerated rates in this group, especially those with chronic conditions. Surprisingly, this current generation of seniors' worst fear is not sudden death; it's becoming disabled and needing complete care.

The question then becomes, what can be done to maintain an active and independent lifestyle? How do you increase your odds of dodging life-threatening or disabling diseases? Most aging advocates agree that having a vibrant lifestyle gives you the best chance of avoiding developmental problems.

The first thing you need to know is that advanced agers, or Super-Agers (80+), often fall into three categories:

1. Survivors
2. Delayers
3. Escapers

All three categories represent individuals who survive a menacing occurrence, delay a severe health event to much later in life, or escape an end-of-life incident. Getting through these monumental issues is, in many ways, miraculous. In the long term, their ability to either maintain, restore, or rehabilitate themselves back to everyday life or close to it becomes more meaningful.

Suffice it to say that these Super-Agers mitigate and recuperate from life-threatening events, successfully extending their living years. What makes these individuals so resilient? Is it just luck, chance, or destiny? Or is it because they made good choices?

Almost all people would like to think that they'll grow old with dignity and be able to take care of themselves for the great majority of their lives. That sounds great, but most people do not attempt to have a long-term productive aging plan. They live day to day, week to week, month to month, and so on. They say, "if something happens, it happens; we'll just deal with it then." I call them the "whatever" people you know the type.

These individuals tend to believe they are reasonably healthy and fit, then suddenly, without warning, they face an unforeseen trauma or disease. I know it's hard to understand, but these creeping aging issues are typically cryptic and insidious, then spontaneously occur. As you read this book, we'll explain why and how these things happen. More importantly, we explain why it's essential to identify these early problems.

There is a riddle that most older adults grow to understand. What runs, and runs, and runs, and never stops? Answer: A Clock! Most aging people, especially seniors, know the clock is relentless.

How often have you heard these cliches spoken?

"Seems like yesterday."

"It happened in the flash of an eye."

"Life is so short."

"I woke up one day, and I was old."

Wouldn't it be better for Aging individuals to look back and reply?

"After all these years, I'm still doing that!"

<u>In contrast to:</u>

"I wish I did that before I got old."

"I wish I could do that."

Other congruent joint aging statements become apropos: *I lost a step! I'm losing my fastball! I'm not what I used to be! Everything is going south!*

Everyone has heard these statements, and most aging individuals can directly relate to them. The bad news is that everyone will lose some of their physicality, and the good news is that most, if not all, of the lost skills, can be rebuilt.

Toby Keith got it right in his song, "I ain't as good as I once was, but I'm as good once as I ever was."

I love that saying because it relates to maintaining skills. Aging reality may say that you're older, but that doesn't mean that you can't continue to achieve, at an age-adjusted high level, if you diligently work at your chosen activity or skill. Having the right attitude will improve your chances.

Prominent Aging Theories

Authors use many terms to define aging, and finding a consensus is difficult. Direct questions arise as to why and when we age. Many shared ideas and new evolving hypotheses are currently being researched and periodically presented.

Here is a sampling of a few of the most prevalent concepts and theories:

1. Dr. August Weismann first introduced the wear and tear theory in 1882. Its basic message is that changes associated with aging are the result of damage that accumulates over time. Like tires on a car, they simply wear out after a certain number of miles.
2. Dr. Denham Harmon proposed the free radical theory in 1956. This theory suggests that oxidative stress impairs and damages body synchrony, eventually leading to aging due to cell damage. These physical breakdowns will cause an accumulation of dangerous decay, eventually overwhelming the system.
3. M. Treisman created a model for time behavior due to an internal clock in 1963. The internal clock formulation gives the impression that age is simply programmed, pre-determined, and preset. "It's just your time!"
4. Elizabeth Blackburn discovered the nature of telomeres and, along with colleagues, received the Nobel Prize in 2009. The telomere theory states that shortening telomeres (a stretch of D.N.A. at the end of a chromosome) during cell division causes cell senescence (the cell no longer replicates). This end process (stagnation) means that there are only so many cycles of cell division in the system. If cell reproduction stops, old cells get defective, and disease processes begin.
5. Jicun Wang and Thomas Michelitsch proposed the mis-repair-accumulation theory in 1995. They suggested that aging results from the accumulation of "disrepair." This theory is essential in distinguishing between "damage," which means a newly emerging defect before any reparation has occurred, and "mis-

repair," which describes the remaining defective structure after incomplete and incorrect healing.

What these theories tell us:

a. Aging will inevitably cause cellular breakdowns leading to death.
b. These opinions demonstrate a pre-programmed time frame (back to the clock). These suppositions refer to aging interactions causing repair processes and cumulative damage.
c. All theories reinforce a survival of the species construct but result in the accumulation of secondary problems causing aging physical losses.

These theories are imperfect as they do not answer our earlier inquiries on how, when, and what causes this aging phenomenon?

Super-Aging addresses the issue of irregular aging by laying out a behavioral construct that allows individuals to continue maintaining an active, productive, and consistent lifestyle with only minimal changes in physical, cognitive, and social interactions. Chronological age does not always reflect biological age, and, with the right mindset, calendar age and bodily changes could be very different. In other words, regardless of personal years lived, your life can continue to maintain, evolve, and in some areas, even grow.

Physical Medicine: The Wonder Drug of Our Time

We use many terms to describe how well we age, such as:

- Healthy Aging
- Successful Aging
- Active Aging
- Thriving while Aging
- And now, Super-Aging

These terms essentially mean one thing; maintaining a vibrant lifestyle leads to better health, including but not limited to the absence of disease and disability. The commonalities of these terms are similar in that they connote a person's ability to maintain their quality of life well into their later years.

Super-Aging distinguishes itself by emphasizing preventative programs which limit physical losses and at the same time preserve the quality of life through compartmentalized exercise and activity (exercise medicine). This exercise for life commitment should focus on fundamental health parameters such as cardiovascular endurance, muscular strength, muscular endurance, flexibility, balance, and body fat. Most importantly, it should address each person's weaknesses.

Complete rehabilitation is imperative in minimizing progressive, cumulative disease and dysfunction. Everyone has inherent weaknesses, and it's important to remember this meaningful proverb, "You're only as strong as your weakest link." This foundational principle will be discussed later in this book.

It's impressive how Exercise Medicine combined with active lifestyles and fully completed rehabilitation has become the wonder drug of our time. Exercise medicine can address medical problems using professionally prescribed, person-specific exercise programs to reduce age-related physical losses. Understanding the importance of controlling weak links is crucial in navigating lifelong disease and injury processes.

Aging Factors That Are Inevitable

It's undeniable that physical, cognitive, and social activity, combined with exercise medicine and training, is the driving force that allows healthy, productive lifestyles. Currently, many researchers cite "inactivity" as one of the top risk factors in disease development. Super-Aging is not about living life as a young person; it's about living life as a regular everyday person who is relatively free of disease and injury.

Just because you've aged does not mean you have to be old. Aging is multifactorial, meaning; chronological, biological, physical, mental, and social age isn't always in harmony and probably shouldn't be. Maintaining a consistent lifestyle is one of the valuable characteristics of Super-Agers. There is no doubt that common pathologies happen progressively and concurrently over our lifespans. Unfortunately, numerous body-mind breakdowns will occur because of the aging process. All are in some ways part of aging, yet in many other forms are part of a process that can be manageable, repairable, and possibly even curable.

If being an active person means extended periods of good health, social engagement, productivity, and independence, and being inactive means having a higher risk for illness, disability, and growing dependency, which destiny would you choose? No brainer, right?

We have all seen the mixed results of current treatment plans after significant injury, surgery, or disease. Many medical procedures do not address long-term recoveries leading to progressive loss of some physical skills. This lack of complete recovery creates a high risk for further decay, future disability, and assisted care.

Knowing that medical systems cannot address the millions of ongoing issues, everyone must take it upon themselves to complete the cycle of restoring full function. It's integral to realize that procedures are not complete until you are back to pre-injury, pre-disease status, or making progress towards this state.

Incomplete rehabilitation can be a precursor to long-term problems, leading to chronic conditions. As most people find out throughout their lives, "s*it happens." How we adapt to the constant rigors of life will eventually determine our ability to control and sustain a valuable and productive way of existing.

CHAPTER 3: Aging Truisms, Falsehoods, Myths, and Mysteries

How often have you sat around a dinner table or another get-together and discussed the latest health, fitness, diet, and treatment trends? Next time you attend one of these gatherings, ask someone who looks healthy and fit what they're doing to stay in shape or what kind of new strategy they're trying? Try saying, "How do you stay so young?" or "You look great for your age." Now that you've primed the conversation, get ready to hear someone's personal opinions, assorted viewpoints, maybe some reasonable suggestions, but most likely, speculative beliefs.

Almost everyone has a thought process about what those around them should do to keep looking and feeling young and energized. Those people don't necessarily do what they're professing to others, but they swear they know what to do. With the limitless number of viewpoints, how do we filter through all these testimonials?

News programs, health and fitness organizations, food and drug companies, and social media influencers continuously push their newest revolutionary, anti-aging, health, and wellness products. Research institutions repeatedly tell us that they're on the verge of curing significant diseases, decreasing pain, improving vitality, and extending lives. Are these extravagant assertions factual, half-truths, misleading, or are they primarily made for economic reasons? How do we know what to believe?

Regretfully, there are many theories, fabrications, anecdotes, and even folklore presented depicting "so-called" facts. What's presumably true about anti-aging is often based on something heard, read, personal and family experiences, or simply opinion! Some practical information shows trends, but actual evidence is scarce.

Optimistic vs. Pessimistic Aging Mindsets

How does the average person view aging? Is it simply the process of growing older? Optimists describe aging as a process that leads to enhanced experience, skill, knowledge, and wisdom (not to mention some great discounts)! In contrast, pessimists feel obligated to state the obvious negative aging connotations, including consistent cellular breakdown, which leads to decay, weakness, deterioration, and eventual death.

I'm sure optimists will be positively encouraged with the questions below, knowing that the answers will help them deal with future problems. For the doubters with an opposing viewpoint, maybe we can change their mindset from skeptic to at least the perspective that you have nothing to lose by trying. Either way, let's answer these questions to inform, educate, and explore ways to reduce detrimental aging changes.

- When does aging start?
- How does it progress?
- Can it be modified or controlled?
- Is there a way to slow it down?

Since there is tremendous ambiguity and equivocation about aging, many investigators will explore all reports that may appear probable, plausible, or even remotely possible. As a result, suppositions based on inconclusive information have become somewhat routine. This copious amount of speculative data leads us to conclude that there continues to be a shortage of bonified, well-accepted, objective, and nonpartisan aging realities.

Truisms: Accepted Actualities

Let's talk about some rational facts and practical truisms. For instance, some conclusive aging changes will happen to everyone over time. Does everyone universally accept this statement as an intractable truth? An overwhelming majority do, but I guarantee you there are people out there who would beg to differ. In our presentation of a truism, we will be as precise and accurate as possible using only well-documented and well-accepted truths.

Knowing that there are creatures on this planet with extended lifespans (hydra, sponges, and jellyfish), the aging oracles remain optimistic about their future projections. Their logic is if other lifeforms can live longer lives, so can human beings. The unfortunate truth is that current experimentation with worms, flies, mice, and other research animals, is still unreliable when contrasting the aging probabilities in human beings.

Rather than dealing with the possibility of infinite life, we focus on the historical knowledge of what has happened to human beings over the past few thousand years. Speculation is way more fun, but we'll stick to as-old-as-time facts in this presentation!

When aging starts is highly debated, but general agreement is that these transformations begin somewhere around the late 20s or early 30s. This phenomenon is unquestionably individualized, distinct, and unpredictable. Only one thing that aging researchers almost universally agree on is that aging is a paradox, incredibly uncertain, perplexing, and consistently inconsistent!

Here is a simple, all-encompassing interpretation: aging represents the average point in peoples' lives where breakdown exceeds buildup. So, what does that mean? Does anyone know if they're still building up? Alternatively, do we know if or when we started breaking down?

For most people, it's probably an assumption, belief, or simply estimation. The point is that you're probably guessing how you're aging based solely on your current health and fitness status. We respect everyone's right to have an opinion, but our goal, in this section is to be as accurate as possible.

Before we begin identifying truisms, we must mention that there's probably nothing that we document that can't be argued in some way. In today's world of incredible advancement, an absolute is hard to find. Let's qualify by saying as of 2021; these truths are quantified with consensus agreement. We will also include virtual truisms that align with reality but do not entirely adhere to strict definitions.

Our Top 10 List of Aging Truisms, Including Our Top 5 and 5 From the World Health Organization

Super-Aging's Top 5

Truism No.1: Every Person Will Age - Somehow, Someway, Guaranteed

This first truism is not debatable (barring diehard fountain of youth advocates), no one defeats time, and everyone will age, no matter what. Aging is a universal phenomenon. Unfortunately, aging will ultimately affect every bodily system. All our senses will become compromised, including vision, hearing, taste, touch, and smell. Arteries stiffen, bladder control diminishes, and sexual drive decreases. Muscle mass shows a gradual decline. Bones lose mineral content. Metabolism is slowed, along with reflexes, leading to reduced physical skill. Internal organs are less efficient and lose elasticity and strength.

Truism No 2: Aging Is the Most Significant Risk Factor for Human Disease

These aging processes contribute to a greater risk of breakdown and create an environment ripe for developing disease-causing issues. The good news is that many of these problems are manageable and don't necessarily lead to a compromised lifestyle.

Truism No. 3: Fitness and Health Is Not Age-Dependent

The third important truism is that aging individuals in their 60s-90s, and even people over 100, can and do make remarkable progress with fitness and health parameters. Here's an aging truth to ponder: "It's not how old you are in years; it's how old you are in terms of health and fitness."

Truism No. 4: There's an Abundance of Factors That Contribute to Injury and Disease That Are Not Age-Related

How often have you heard or thought to yourself that my issues are age-related? You may have even said to yourself, "I'm just getting old!" Maybe that's the case, or perhaps it's something else. Is it about aging or a breakdown due to your individualized issues or other extenuating circumstances? In the coming chapters, we extensively discuss the innumerable amount of possible disease and injury mechanisms.

Truism No 5: Older People Who Think They Are Doing Better, More Times Than Not, Do Better

The point is: Never Stop Believing! Those who have a positive outlook can walk faster, are more likely to recover from severe disability, and best yet, live an average of seven and a half years longer. This fact is fascinating and reported by many aging researchers and authors.

Top 5 Fundamental Truths Put Out by the WHO

No. 1: There Is NO Typical Older Person

Mature age groups are grossly different in so many ways. Some eighty-year-olds are running marathons, while others in this age group are dependent. Enormous differences in the elderly population make it imperative not to prejudge living capacities and special needs secondary to age. As the writer and activist Ashton Applewhite said, "If you've seen one 80-year-old, you've seen one 80-year-old."

No. 2: Diversity in Older Age Is Not Random

Many variables revolve around aging, including class, sex, race, education, and mindset. Gracefully growing old is also potentiated by a host of other factors, including being social, autonomous, optimistic, motivated, and how and where you live. All of this, and other intangibles, affects aging. We entirely cover aging factors in the preceding chapters.

No. 3: Only A Small Proportion of Older Adults Are Care-Dependent

The truth is that most seniors can take care of themselves without assistance well into their later years. Only 10% of seniors over 85 live in nursing homes, and those individuals are mostly living without help.

No. 4: Seventy is Not the New Sixty

Most seniors tend to believe that they are healthier than previous generations and WHO reports that there has been no significant change in reported disabilities in the past 30 years. Hopefully, this independence trend continues, but lifestyle changes, especially inactivity and unhealthy weight, have created a higher risk for injury and disease, accelerating premature aging. I love the optimism coming from current seniors. Still, reality says that the present-day 70-year-old may not be more youthful than their parents and grandparents and may face more significant future challenges.

No. 5: Families Are Essential, but Contemporary Generations Believe That They Alone Cannot Provide the Care Many Older People Need

Caring for aging family members in the USA and other first-world countries is no longer the norm. Accessory health care groups are expanding exponentially, and direct care from family members is contracting. Aging individuals are being forced to decide what type of care they desire (outside of family), if needed, in later life dependency circumstances. This evolving situation makes maintaining independence a priority goal in the aging community.

Falsehoods

Falsehoods are general depictions with some circumstantial validity (can happen) but are not factual overall, making them dangerous statements that can cause faulty perceptions leading to poor decisions. No one should make an important choice based on falsehoods.

Falsehood No. 1: Aging Is a Disease!

Is aging a process or a disease? We believe it's far more accurate to describe aging as a process. Explicitly speaking, diseases mostly align with short-term illnesses, sicknesses, disorders, and other spontaneous treatable ailments. Aging relates to generalized lifelong decay, deterioration, and incremental stepwise changes over time, causing increased vulnerability to many different medical problems and conditions.

Falsehood No.2: Miracle Cures Are Imminent

Current forms of mass media have produced an incredible amount of propaganda. Anti-aging falsehoods and miracle cures are everywhere! Suffice it to say; there are far more snake oil salespeople today than at any other time in history. Perhaps some person, entity, or company will prove us wrong soon, but at this point, groundbreaking cures for our biggest killers are, most likely, not imminent.

Falsehood No. 3: Dementia Is a Normal or Inevitable Part of Aging

Growing old does not automatically mean becoming senile, and early-onset dementia can be treated and should be considered a medical condition. Those dreaded senior moments, especially forgetfulness, are far more likely to be caused by diet, apathy, psycho-social issues, or the number one cause, medications. Most Gerontologists believe that at age 65, only roughly 5% of elders will be experiencing senility, and this number slowly climbs to approximately 20% by age 85. That means 80% of our seniors won't have dementia.

Falsehood No. 4: Arthritic Joints Are Inevitable

Although most elders will experience different degrees of conclusive deterioration, there is no need to panic, as many cases of arthritis are treatable. Don't fall prey to negative expectations and projections. Arthritis does not have to be a sentence to progressive breakdown and eventual surgical treatment.

Falsehood No. 5: You're Too Old to Do the Rehabilitation

This statement is not only false but also dangerous. It is well documented that older adults can make remarkable improvements when completing rehabilitation programs lasting approximately 8-10 weeks. Remarkably, even the most elderly populations have shown tremendous improvement of strength and function using supervised rehabilitation and training programs.

Falsehood No.6: It's All About the Genes

Many people believe that an individual's genes are responsible for healthy aging. While there is no doubt that genes are an essential factor in advancing years, it's false to think that your lineage and ancestry will guarantee you a long life. WHO recently published (May 1, 2017) their "Top ten fact list on Aging."? Number nine on that list states, "It's not all about the genes; only twenty-five percent of our health is from our genes." When discussing lifespans, many other factors like diet, physical activity, exposure to chemicals, lifestyles, and stress are equally important, or in many ways, more important than genes.

Falsehood No. 7: Seniors Don't Need as Much Sleep

Sadly, seniors have problems sleeping because of numerous medical and non-medical issues. Why seniors are not sleeping is usually multifactorial and, if extreme, should be investigated. Many researchers believe lack of sleep or too much sleep is a risk factor.

Others believe that poor sleep patterns manifest other medical issues, secondarily causing disrupted rest. Seniors' need for sleep is unchanged and remains vitally essential throughout life. Non-Sleepers should consider adding weekly physical activity to their life. The BMJ (2021, June 29) states high physical activity levels may counter serious health harms of poor sleep.

Falsehood No. 8: Old Age Results in Total Loss of Libido

Libido decreases, but many older individuals continue to maintain satisfying relationships. Younger adults may wince when they hear this, but a good percentage of grandmas and grandpas can and do retain their carnal knowledge well into their later years.

Falsehood No. 9: Osteoporosis Is Inevitable

Most people believe that everyone will have osteoporosis if they live long enough. There is no doubt that osteoporosis is more common in older adults, but, in most cases, it is preventable, or at the very least, treatable.

Falsehood No. 10: Growing Old Means Accepting Loss of Independence, Leading to Complete Care

A primary misconception is that growing old eventually means losing independence, resulting in complete care. At this point, there is no conclusive evidence that most elderly individuals will need some living assistance or comprehensive full-time dependent care. Most healthcare organizations now report that only a tiny portion of the elderly (10-15%) need dependent care.

Growing old does not have to mean you're destined to become sick, disabled, unable to take care of yourself, and then die. It's undoubtedly true that eventually, life's time clock will catch up with you but hopefully, with the right attitude, a healthy lifestyle, and a little luck, you'll be able to take care of yourself for most of your life, if not your entire lifetime.

Myths: Misrepresentations, Legends, and Mistaken Beliefs

Myths are like falsehoods, but they develop over decades, centuries, and even millennia. Myths are innumerable and subject to anyone's imagination. Famed storytellers weave epic tales that are awe-inspiring, uplifting and depict incredible feats and odysseys. In contrast, harmful myths are often degrading, destructive, and dehumanizing. Believing these dangerous misrepresentations can lead to preemptive, contradictory, and irrational behavior.

Myth No. 1: The Older I Get, the Sicker I Will Become

Many believe the older you get, the sicker you will become. This statement is somewhat true but, like all myths, is an exaggeration. Everyone gets ill but how each person recovers from sickness is highly variable. How you've led your life, and not your age, will determine your ability to fight off disease and get back to normal. It's not about being sick and getting sicker as you get older. It's about getting ill and recovering because you're healthy.

Myth No. 2: Physical Activity Is Harmful to Seniors

The notion that physical activity is harmful to seniors is the most threatening myth of all! The literature is replete with conclusive evidence that many risk factors (including premature mortality) can not only be reduced, controlled, and forestalled with active lifestyles. Almost always, physical activity is not only not hazardous but also the preeminent foundation for maintaining mobile and productive lives.

Myth No. 3: Urinary Incontinence Is a Normal Part of Aging

Unfortunately, urinary incontinence is a growing problem that affects approximately 50% of senior women and 25% of senior men. It's not necessarily a normal part of aging, but it disproportionately affects older individuals. An essential factor is that UI is highly treatable. It's imperative to understand that growing weakness and obesity contribute significantly to UI. Doing pelvic floor movements (Kegels) and associated abdominal, groin, and trunk exercises can help eliminate or control symptoms. So again, physical deficits rather than age could be the most significant constituent of the problem.

Myth No. 4: Aches and Pains Are Unavoidable for the Elderly

While aches and pains may not be avoidable, they're not always caused by aging. Aches and pains are categorically different from person to person. Some seniors have joint-specific, regional pain or multi-area tenderness, while others have generalized soreness, and some are symptom-free. Body aches and pains are conflicting, with many distinct causes and etiologies. You may resolve these aches and pain by addressing specific signs and symptoms.

Myth No. 5: Older People Are Destined to Be Lonely and Depressed

There is no doubt that some aging individuals are subject to short or long-term loneliness and depression. The loss of close friends and loved ones, beginning retirement, and having disabilities are contributing factors. Loneliness and depression are not destiny but perhaps a choice in many cases. It's often not because you're old; it's because you've isolated yourself. Actively making time to stay involved with family, friends, and community is a significant factor in staying engaged and healthy into old age.

Myth No. 6: You're Going to Lose All of Your Teeth

Dental disease is not a normal part of aging, although many seniors have poor dental health. Periodontal disease is often caused by hard brushing, poor hygiene, smoking, dry mouth issues, and poor food choices. New techniques have made tooth loss more treatable. You are not destined to lose your teeth if you practice prevention first and regularly visit your dentist. Oral health problems, like tooth loss and gum disease, are associated with an increased risk of frailty. If you take care of your teeth, you can probably delay or prevent extensive treatment.

Myth No. 7: All Seniors Eventually Become Frail

Only a tiny percentage (3.9%) of the elderly from 65-74 become frail, and typical ranges in the 85 plus group are 7-12%. In most cases, people gradually become weak, experience significant weight loss, and are fragile, feeble, delicate, slowed, and tired, leading to poor health. If you take away end-of-life individuals with severe disease, frailty is primarily developmental and almost always treatable. Fragility is ordinarily a secondary problem and is not an eventuality for most seniors.

Myth No. 8: Older Workers Are Less Efficient Than Younger Workers

We understand why people believe that younger workers are more efficient, but it's not hard to explain why this is a myth and not a reality. The younger generation has more vim and vigor, but work activities are not competitive. Most older workers are more dependable, consistent, reliable, and dedicated. When given the opportunity, older workers are often more efficient than younger workers doing the same job.

Myth No. 9: Most Seniors Will Live in Poverty

Most seniors (50+) not only do not live their lives in poverty, but they are the key drivers of economic growth. The AARP reports that Americans 50 and over constitute the world's third-largest economy. The 50-plus subset of people supports 88.6 million jobs secondary to their spending habits and their long-term employment in the workforce. Only about 11.6 percent of people 80 and above live their life in poverty.

Far too many people believe these falsehoods and myths. Predictably, those believers are most likely to be overcome by them. Our advice is not to get caught up in exaggerated, foreboding, irrational, and pessimistic thinking patterns. Anything and everything can and often does happen to all age groups in life. If you're going to believe in myths, choose positive ones.

While we can't always explain why negative expectations often produce negative results, it's not surprising when this negativity develops; unfavorable outcomes follow. If you think something will happen to you, it probably will. Remember, most myths are the exception and not the rule.

Mysteries

The definition of mystery is a circumstance or occurrence that is difficult or impossible to understand or explain. Mysteries are incomprehensible, puzzling, and ambiguous. Aging mysteries are unusually distinct because they revolve around promising perceptions and optimism but, in many ways, are unrealistic and far-fetched probabilities.

There are endless conversations about aging mysteries due to wonder, curiosity, and the allure of something not known or poorly understood. Almost everybody chimes in on these conversations because there's no right or wrong answer. Let's talk about some of these aging discussions and debates.

Mystery No 1: Is the Length of Life Increasing or Unchanged?

When discussing total years lived, theories abound, debating the seemingly limitless possibilities. Some of these include increasing the expected life span to over 100 years, possibly even hundreds of years. Some researchers are even debating immortality! You can make up your mind on what you want to believe is possible, but at this point, the oldest female in history was Jeanne Calment (France) lived 122 years from 1875-to 1997. The most aged male, Jiroemon Kimura (Japan), lived 116 years from 1897-to 2013.

Exuberant optimism surrounds an increasing length of life. Still, the reality is that lifespan has not changed in human history, and we believe that the entire length of life won't change any time soon. Just so there's no confusion, lifespan (possible total years) is unchanged, but more people live longer (average length of life) than at any time in recorded history. So, for our purposes, we will stick with the current average lifespan in the USA of approximately 77 years for men and 80 years for women.

Mystery No 2: How Do Lifestyles and Environment Affect Aging? Does What You Eat, Drink, Smoke, and Supplements or Medications You Take Affect Aging, and if So, In What Way?

All the above absolutely can affect aging! It's impossible to determine how and to what extent these variables affect individuals. Unequivocally, smoking, drinking, poor eating patterns, and drug use can become dependency problems. These addictions accelerate health risks, often tragically.

Mystery No 3: Do Single Events Influence Aging?

You certainly would think so, but remember the old cliché, "What doesn't kill you makes you stronger." Don't take this statement the wrong way. We are not endorsing overzealous behavior; we're just acknowledging some merit to well-established overload principles. Challenging nature is a staple of resistance training and sports. Are we building up the body and testing nature's limits, or are we tearing ourselves apart? All we can say is, be cautious when crossing that perilous line of risk versus reward!

Mystery No 4: What Causes Aging Issues Such as Heart Disease, Osteoarthritis, Diabetes, or Dementia, and What Can We Do to Inhibit or Control Progression?

Most gerontologists believe that these conditions are mainly developmental, which may be manageable. We will discuss and explore all these aging pathologies in upcoming chapters.

Mystery No 5: Is There Anything We Can Do to Help Withstand Disease?

If you educate yourself on risk factors, you can suppress aging through healthy living, staying lean, total body conditioning, being mentally and physically active, and having good judgment. These steps can be protective and may save someone's life!

Mystery No 6: Is Aging Treatable in All Age Groups?

Aging is treatable, period. You are never too old to recover, restore, or rehabilitate! While there are untreatable conditions, this mindset, especially from healthcare professionals, that you're too old to receive comprehensive treatment is often based on erroneous pre-conceived beliefs. We believe that the type of treatment the elderly receive should be determined case-by-case. A qualified physician or therapist should evaluate every aging person based on their physical status and rehabilitation potential and not on their age.

Current and Future Aging Theories, Research, and Treatment

This section will discuss current and future aging theories, research, and treatments. Which therapeutic approach will be proven to suppress or reduce aging losses? Now that's a real mystery! We will sub-divide our discussion into rejuvenation, replacement surgeries or organ transplants, and regenerative medicine.

We do not include popular diets, creams, food sources, and the innumerable amount of other advertised anti-aging products because they are too numerous to discuss.

1. **Rejuvenation:** Treatments designed to restore the quality of life or simply feel younger.

   a. Antioxidants: They work to combat free radicals that inflict cell damage (vitamin A, E, and enzyme proteins) and, in turn, counter the harmful by-products of oxygenation.
   b. Heat shock proteins: These proteins are produced by the body during periods of stress. These components then aid cells to dismantle and dispose of other damaged proteins. Their therapeutic application shows promise, and development is being pursued.
   c. Caloric restrictions: Caloric restrictions have been shown to delay the onset of age-related diseases and declines. Intriguing and plausible new research continues.
   d. Resveratrol: Resveratrol is found in grapes and wine. It has been shown to decrease heart-related problems and increase bone health, balance, and motor function. It can be absorbed through diet or supplementation. Beware, wine consumers, this is not an excuse to drink more wine; only one to two drinks are the recommended norm!
   e. Rapamycin: This prescription medication helps suppress the immune system, which aids the mTOR pathway to control the rate of protein synthesis. This drug is promising but has numerous side effects. Consult with your physician or pharmacist.
   f. Telomerase: Telomerase is an enzyme that helps restore telomere reproduction and extends cell life. This additive is available as a supplement.
   g. Body Sculpting and Plastic Surgeries: Numerous methods are used to reshape an area of your body. These procedures also include fat reduction techniques.
   h. Blood transfusion: These procedures have been extensively researched and are typically used to revitalize individuals with younger plasma and red blood cells. Dracula would be proud!

i. <u>Hormones</u>: Human growth hormone (HGH), testosterone, estrogen/progesterone, and other testosterone boosters. These products are mostly prescription drugs, and they tend to improve strength, muscle, bone mass, and sex drive. Side effects are a subject of tremendous debate.

j. <u>Injections</u>: A specialized mix of toxins and medications is now used to reduce wrinkles and treat musculoskeletal conditions.

k. All the above aging agents have shown some measure of success, but most have numerous associated implications. Super-Aging does not recommend or give treatment advice, but we will say to do your homework before trying any one of these anti-aging methods.

2. **Replacement Surgeries and Organ Transplants**: Revolutionary procedures to "restore" the quality of living or save lives.

a. <u>Joint replacements surgeries:</u> These have become somewhat mainstream. A million-plus of these procedures are routinely done each year, with the hip, knee, and shoulder being the most common. Efficacy and long-term results are discussed later in this book.

b. <u>Donor organ transplants:</u> These are also becoming typical. The heart, lung, liver, pancreas, cornea, trachea, skin, and kidney are most usual. As always, if there are options available, we recommend thorough investigation and consultation with numerous practitioners and trusted family members and friends before moving forward.

3. **Regenerative Medicine**: Involves regrowing, repairing, or replacing damaged or diseased cells, organs, or tissue. This branch of science includes but is not limited to tissue engineering, biomaterials, cellular therapies, medical devices, and artificial organs. These methods are undoubtedly the most futuristic and visionary areas of medicine with unlimited potential to improve the quality of life. Here are four of the primary therapies:

a. <u>Prolotherapy:</u> Involves injecting a natural irritant into a soft tissue area to increase inflammation, which, in turn, stimulates a healing response.

b. <u>Platelet Rich Plasma (PRP):</u> This technique works by drawing blood from a patient spinning it to withdraw growth factor-rich platelets, then reinjecting back into the patients' diseased area. Theoretically, this should then enhance and promote healing.

c. Senolytic Drugs: A relatively new pharmaceutical agent designed to delay, prevent, alleviate, or reverse age-related diseases. They selectively destroy senescent cells (dormant cells), improving human health. Many researchers believe that this drug will be the next great medicine for improved health.

d. Stem Cells: Used to replace or rejuvenate damaged tissue using a procedure to withdraw blood from a vein or bone marrow, harvest stem cells, and then reinfuse them into the diseased area. Extensive research is also being done investigating other potential uses for growing tissues, organs, and other vital structures.

Aging mysteries, in our view, are probably the most engaging and captivating topic for discussion. Researchers worldwide are trying to unlock age-old secrets to life-threatening, life-extending, and life genesis possibilities. Rejuvenation is our favorite because it offers ways to invigorate someone's life so they can continue to live in a usual way. Replacement procedures represent critical lifetime losses necessitating major surgery to replace those unrepairable structures. Later in this book, Super-Aging explores ways to prevent those losses. Regenerative medicine is the most interesting because of its limitless potential. What does the future hold?

This chapter on truths, falsehoods, myths, and mysteries was written to help people decipher the incredible amount of misinformation circulating in public arenas. Navigating through the tsunami of possibilities is a daunting task. If you understand aging realities, you'll realize that it's possible to grow old and maintain a normal lifestyle if you commit to reducing aging losses. If society can continue to lengthen our life span, we must also develop ways to extend our associated health span.

CHAPTER 4: Modifiable vs. Non-Modifiable Risk Factors

One of the main themes of this book is to alert people to aging factors that lead to an increased probability of having a lowered standard of living. The twentieth century saw tremendous changes in epidemiology (the branch of medicine that deals with the incidence, distribution, and possible control of diseases). Life-threatening illness has transitioned from infectious, to acute, to chronic, and in today's world, degenerative disease has become the primary cause of aging disorders.

Chronic illness or injury (three or more months) means that your issue is long-standing but not necessarily lifelong. In contrast, degenerative disease is developmental and happens over years and decades. With dedicated perseverance, some of these harmful changes and vicious cycles can be altered or even reversed with lifestyle changes or treatment. This transformation is imperative to understand because infectious and acute diseases happen spontaneously and result in immediate or imminent issues and sometimes death.

This chapter discusses the risk factors that commonly lead to these disorders, predisposing people to compromised lifestyles. A risk factor refers to something that increases a person's chances of developing a problem, and that risk could be biological, chemical, physical, psychological, personal, or due to something else.

Super-Aging believes that these budding factors should be subdivided into early formational issues versus complex late-stage problems and conditions. Early risk factors lead to escalating problems, leading to formational breakdowns. We will repeatedly say this throughout this book because of its monumental importance! If you control early elements, you consequently lessen incubating looming diseases.

Perennial diseases are quickly becoming the norm in senior populations. The National Institute of Health has reported that 60% of older adults have at least two or more chronic diseases.

Here Is a Top 10 List of Common Chronic Conditions:

1. Back and Neck pain
2. Arthritis

3. Extended and Lifelong Obesity
4. Respiratory Issues
5. Diabetes (type 2)
6. Hypertension
7. Heart Disease
8. Stroke Survivors
9. Cancer
10. Dementia (Alzheimer's)

All these conditions above are examples of complex late-stage issues. Four of these conditions, arthritis, diabetes, long-term obesity, and Alzheimer's, have shown an unprecedented, startling rise. Why is this happening, and why is it becoming so common? Can we reduce or control these conditions by understanding what is causing them (early risk)?

The simple answer is that although we now live longer lives, our fitness and health have declined partially due to addictive behavior and sedentary lifestyles. The result is a prolific rise in the diseases mentioned above. Let's remember our specific definition of aging, the progressive loss of vital tissue, physical skill, essential capacities, and associated function. By knowing early risk factors, you can take the necessary steps to preclude, change, or treat these conditions before they incubate into challenging disease issues.

If you allow health issues to develop, the chance of experiencing compromised living also increases. If that's not bad enough, many of these people can be victimized by tragic events, including an alarming rise in premature deaths. Remember, Super-Agers have minimal to no chronic problems, and that factor alone significantly reduces the chances of catastrophic events. Sure, anything can happen, but the point is that many of these life-ending situations can be repressed.

Premature Deaths:

Regrettably, many individuals won't ever get to see their retirement years. Age-related changes can begin at any time in your life, and these changes could put you at high risk of suffering a life-threatening event. What can society do to avert or forestall the high incidence of premature deaths?

According to the Centers for Disease Control, devastating incidents continue to happen at alarming rates. Regrettably, the untold, barely mentioned story is that many end-of-life occurrences can often be counteracted. The CDC says that 15% of cancer deaths, 28% of stroke deaths, 30% of heart disease deaths, 36% of chronic respiratory deaths, and a whopping 43% of accidental deaths can be diminished. These numbers are incomprehensible but true.

Families are traumatized when a loved one leaves this planet early. Additionally, many others are overwhelmed if they believe they could have saved someone from these life-ending departures by changing their circumstances. Let's explore what individuals can do to decrease the high incidence of these developmental issues, including premature deaths.

Non-Modifiable Risk Factors (Factors You Have Minimal or No Control Over)

What are the non-modifiable risk factors that lead to high-risk situations? Many people believe that their lot in life is predetermined. A familiar statement is, "you can't pick your parents." In other words, your heredity, genetic makeup, and biological traits are unchangeable; they are decided at birth. Does that mean that you can do nothing about hereditary disease factors?

It's undoubtedly true that some people are victims of genetic predisposition potentiating the development of chronic issues and possibly life-threatening disorders. It's also true that, in many cases, newer treatments, psycho-social adaptations, and lifestyle changes can modify, alter, and even preclude previously untreatable conditions. There is no doubt that healthy families have higher occurrences of healthy children, but there are absolutely no guarantees that good genes will result in long healthy lives!

Other factors that are somewhat unpredictable are things like:

- environmental factors
- poor social interactions
- cultural differences
- economic disparities

- geographic anomalies
- education
- poor judgment
- traumatic injury
- infectious agents
- lack of medical care
- inadequate medical care
- medical error

In many ways, non-modifiable factors are intrinsically linked to the age-old argument of nature vs. nurture, now known as epigenetics. What's the more critical issue? How do you lead your life or inherited genes? New research is now documenting that your genes become less imperative, and adaptation is more vital as you age. The jury is still out, but most people believe it's a combination of genes and surroundings. The debate continues.

How we interact, modify, and adapt to living conditions (surroundings) affects gene expression, changing our living probabilities. These changes could ultimately be good or bad. Will varied environmental conditions improve your chances of good health, or will your surroundings escalate the risk for premature disease or injury factors?

Many other non-modifiable factors simultaneously co-exist. We call these factors non-modifiable because, in most cases, you cannot choose where you live, the air you breathe, your encircling social environment, local food sources, educational opportunities, medical networks available, etc. We create an astronomical number of possibilities when we interweave all these variables and their corresponding interactions together. In other words, we all do the best we can under the circumstances we're given.

Undeniably, life is somewhat of a poker game; we have no choice but to play the cards we're dealt. How we play each hand (lifestyle choices) in the long run determines how well we do in the game of life. Non-modifiable conditions are a part of life. The good news is there are also many modifiable things we can do to address the risk of premature medical issues, including death.

Modifiable Risk Factors

Many things in our life are somewhat out of our control. Karma, chance, and destiny are considered by many as formidable foes, but even the staunchest believers agree that modifications are possible. Are you good because you're lucky, or are you lucky because you're good? For conversation purposes, we will let everyone decide this highly debatable question for themselves.

Moving back to reality, everyone should understand that there is an abundance of documented evidence that shows that hundreds of thousands of deaths can be avoidable. Many other diseases and injuries add tens of thousands of other fatalities to this expanding list of early casualties.

Anyone looking at these numbers should be outraged that we are not doing enough to educate people on diminishing the early onset of these disastrous conditions. If these numbers aren't bad enough, just think of the millions of so-called survivors of severe disease, their subsequent poor quality of life, and the effect this has on their families and our healthcare system.

We also feel it's essential to include a special mention to the growing number of individuals with active addictions. These behaviors are now a predominant threat that dramatically accelerates lifestyle dilemmas. In the short run, beware of ill-advised or reckless activity, resulting in accidental trauma. In the long term (months or years), worrisome addictions can ultimately cause life-altering, life-threatening conditions. Even if you can dodge death's doorstep, progressive breakdown, if not changed, leads to declining health conditions and a high risk for an expansive assortment of diseases and dysfunctions.

For individuals who realize they have a severe substance use disorder (SUD) but continue their high-risk behavior, you need to do some real soul searching. Albert Einstein once said this crude but astute observation, "Any fool can know; the point is to understand." If SUD affects your quality of life, it's paramount that you reach out and pursue help from family and friends whenever possible. If family and friends are not available or not responding, seek out professional care or some type of counseling usually available through local, state, or federal organizations. We feel for everyone struggling with addiction and hope they'll find a path toward recovery before something catastrophic happens.

Now, let's discuss some early and late-stage risk factors that can be modified or controlled with awareness and the right mindset. Remember our previous mention about disease development (Epidemiology). Degenerative disease is our leading cause of premature disability and death. If you can reduce early risk factors, you can significantly allay or delay late-stage injuries and diseases. Recognizing these growing dysfunctions can be invaluable in avoiding or decreasing their derogatory effects and progression.

Early Developmental Risk Factors for Injury and Disease:

1. Active addiction: This is discussed above but reviewed here due to its importance. Smoking, drug abuse, and alcoholism are the top three addictions and number one risk factors in life. Smoking is still the leading cause of premature deaths, but drug and alcohol abuse are rising.
2. Inactivity: Sedentary lifestyles are on everyone's list for the top of the class causative factors leading to compromised living. The combination of sitting, lack of exercise, and lack of weight-bearing motion is causing a tremendous loss of functional capacity.
3. Growing losses of muscle, bone, and metabolizing tissue: Although these insidious tissue losses may take many years, controlling these erosions can delay and frequently delay long-term disease and dysfunction.
4. Overeating results in unhealthy weight: BMI levels over 30 have been well documented to contribute to significant illness and injury. Obesity not only contributes to loss of joint integrity and compromised weight-bearing status but is also the main ingredient for developing many life-altering, life-threatening diseases.
5. Unhealthy diet: Poor food choices disproportionally affect long-term health. Overindulgence in food additives, preservatives, and refined foods over time is concerning due to the accumulation of disease-causing by-products. We will further discuss this in upcoming chapters.
6. Stress: High-stress levels contribute to many other disorders. Depression, anxiety, mood swings, and sleeping issues are manifestations of stress. If you control stressors, you can manage many other lurking problems.

7. Physical and Mental Health: Maintaining good physical and mental health is a no-brainer. Accomplishing this is multifactorial and takes tremendous discipline and a consistent lifestyle plan. Stay tuned.

8. Social interaction: Maintaining connections with family, friends, and community aids in the reduction of loneliness and reinforces productive lifestyles. Having an enriching social environment that promotes healthy living is a vital cog in the wheelhouse of life.

9. Occupation: Having a prosperous or satisfying workplace improves the quality of life, and job dissatisfaction is a recipe for growing mental issues.

10. Where you live: Not always manageable, but an enriching environment is a real plus when trying to lead a rewarding life.

Late-Stage Complex Risk Factors that Customarily Result in Treatment:

1. Heart Disease, Stroke, COPD, and Cancer: These conditions are all listed together because we will thoroughly discuss these problematic issues in the next chapter. Suffice it to say that these diseases can culminate into dangerous disease risk factors.

2. Hypertension, High Cholesterol, and High Blood Sugar (type II diabetes) are precursors to many diseases, especially heart disease and stroke. Reducing and restraining these conditions saves lives.

3. Chronic conditions: Multiple long-term conditions are a recipe for compromised living and shortened lives. In May 2017, the NIH reported that eighty-five percent of older adults have at least one disorder, and sixty percent have two or more ongoing problems. Life is shortened by years for every chronic condition, and there is virtually no disagreement on this consequential fact.

4. Hyper-Obesity: We list this because your risk for all-encompassing physical problems is a virtual guarantee. Extreme internal and external body fat is implicated in numerous biological breakdowns.

5. Frailty: Gross losses of muscle and bone are usually a late-stage terminal situation. Senescence that leads to weakness produces cells that become stagnant and inefficient. Controlling cell loss is an imperfect science, but Super-Agers undoubtedly lose less metabolically active cells through active, productive lifestyles.

6. <u>Immunosuppression:</u> Age-related innate and adaptive immune systems changes are vital in controlling disease-causing problems. Primary causes of reduced immune system capabilities include radiation, chemicals, pathogens, gut microbes, nutritional components, stress, and drug use. That's the shortlist. One of the great mysteries for sustaining life is building up or maintaining a functioning immune system. In the meantime, keeping a healthy body and strong mind works for Super-Agers.

7. <u>Inflammation:</u> Controlling chronic inflammation is a necessity if you want to control aging and its harmful components. Medications are currently being used with less than optimum results, and exercise has been shown to decrease inflammation with proper application. Further investigation into controlling inflammation is a primary goal of researchers.

8. <u>Growing Disability</u>: Like all other late-stage problems, an impairment frequently results from cumulative deterioration. Controlling losses is a fundamental aim of this book. We will cover ways to reduce the probability of disability throughout this book.

9. <u>Fall Risk:</u> Losing the ability to navigate your environment is becoming widespread and overwhelmingly common, leading to tens of thousands of unnecessary traumas, including premature deaths. Reducing these balance issues should be a priority.

10. <u>Medication use</u>: Long-term use of prescriptions has become prevalent, with even double-digit prescribed medications coupled with an ever-expanding number of over-the-counter pharmaceuticals. Chemical interactions and adverse side effects can compromise lifestyles. Some of these medications are lifesavers, but many others may be unnecessary. We will discuss this later in this book.

Understanding the commonalities of our most dreaded diseases, we begin to understand that addictive behavior, inactivity, unhealthy weight, and poor diets are primary players in most conditions. Addressing these early risk factors may decrease the development of other more significant illnesses. Add curbing physical losses and controlling stress, and your chances for advanced disease falls considerably.

Regarding late-stage complex issues, be aware that the familiar precursor diseases, like hypertension, diabetes, and high cholesterol, are the leading causes of heart disease and stroke. Respiratory problems and cancers are also frequently preceded by poor health and environmental exposure to pollutants.

Knowing that only 5% of the population leads a healthy lifestyle is disturbing. We must change our perception of what we consider every day, rewarding life. Our preoccupation with recreational leisure time (especially eating and drinking), along with a growing network of sit-down jobs and activities, has transformed a high percentage of society into unhealthy and unfit individuals with growing complex problems.

We understand that not everyone fits into the exercise and fitness world. Our goal is to promote and provide alternative ways for everyone to continue to live life as normally as possible. Lifestyle changes that encourage more movement, increased social interaction, and cerebral pursuits are accomplishable from all individuals at their own chosen level. We explore many ways to maintain an active and rewarding life in upcoming chapters.

In conclusion, your health risk is exponentially reduced if you don't smoke, remain active, stay lean, control stress, eat a nutritious diet, and control other addictions. These behaviors also help restrain hypertension, high sugar, high cholesterol, and unhealthy weight. The result is that developmental disease and premature death are much less likely.

There are dozens of other significant risk factors to consider depending on your specific individualized habits and circumstances. If you understand your primary issues, you can, alternatively, develop an overall plan to negate risk and improve living. Those steps alone give you an excellent start to a Super-Aging life!

CHAPTER 5: The Big Five Killers in Life

What Are the Risk Factors? Can You Counteract These Potential Tragedies?

Heart disease, cancer, respiratory diseases, strokes, and accidents are major life-threatening issues. Our focus in this chapter is to discuss these threats in the context of premature deaths and shortened lifespans. For decades, life expectancy increased, now new data shows a plateau in the length of life. What is happening in our contemporary world, and what factors account for these changes?

Heart Disease Including Cardio-Vascular-Disease (CVD)

Heart disease has been our most significant contributor to life-changing situations, including premature deaths, since the mid 20th century. Even with prolific advancement and revolutionary new cardiac treatments, heart disease continues to be the leading cause of death globally. Here's an old medical saying, what is your first indication of a heart attack? Death! Sad, but true.

The Center for Disease Control and Prevention (CDC) reports that heart disease kills approximately 647,000 Americans each year. Sudden cardiac death is responsible for about half (or around 320,000 fatalities per year) of all heart disease deaths. These frightening statistics make reducing the incidence of cardiovascular disease a top priority.

Everyone probably knows someone who has suffered from a heart attack. Although most cardiologists believe that heart disease is developmental (happens over years and decades), this disease continues to be our most significant threat to premature issues, including death. Knowing that heart disease persists, can these tragic incidents be delayed, controlled, or suppressed? And if so, what steps should you take, and where should you begin? Great questions -- let's discuss.

We believe starting a heart-smart cardio-vascular endurance program is an excellent place to begin when attempting to lower your risk of heart disease. Along with aerobic exercise, health advocates agree that not smoking, having a healthy weight, eating a nutritionally sound diet, and incorporating resistance exercise routines should be part of a total body approach to combatting heart disease development.

Maintaining social networks is also essential because personal relationships motivate individuals to remain involved in consistent activities and events. We can't emphasize this enough; being a part of something is invaluable. A combination of all these healthy choices reduces the likelihood of CVD.

When Should You See Your Physician?

You must be your own best advocate, but you should also routinely cover your bases using professional health and medical personnel. In the absence of problems, routine physicals every year or two are advisable. Between visits, don't let issues incubate. If you suspect a budding medical condition, make an appointment to investigate. Having a comprehensive history of everything that has happened to you and its treatment is invaluable in assessing future problems.

Understanding the risk factors that lead to heart disease allows for the best chance to lessen premature disease issues. As mentioned in our introduction, most researchers now believe that heart illness is a developmental disease secondary to poor lifestyles. That means that you can impede growing heart problems by controlling high blood pressure, high cholesterol, obesity, diabetes, stress, depression and simultaneously promoting and maintaining lifelong healthy habits.

Dr. Teemu Niiranen said it best (Boston University and Framingham Heart Study), "heart disease is a lifestyle disease." He also noted that staying lean and not developing diabetes are the keys. Other researchers believe that BMI (Body Mass Index) and having more muscle and less fat reduce the risk of early deaths from heart disease. We can't argue with either of these deductions because all these conclusions address the critical components of having a comprehensive exercise program designed to improve health and fitness and reduce disease formation.

Life's Simple Seven

Many medical organizations have similar statements on ways to reduce heart disease. Super-Aging agrees with and endorses this informational paradigm from the American Heart Association (AHA) called "Life's Simple Seven."

1. Keep blood pressure normal
2. Keep cholesterol low
3. Keep blood sugar down
4. Stay active
5. Eat healthily
6. Lose weight
7. Stop or don't smoke

I know that this doesn't sound very simple in practice! So, let's discuss and explain step-by-step ways to address the formation of heart disease.

First: Don't smoke and if you already smoke, try religiously to quit. Next, adhere to sound exercise and diet principles. The chances are good that you probably won't need to worry about high blood pressure, high cholesterol, type two diabetes, or obesity if you establish and maintain healthy living patterns. Lastly, find a doctor that you can communicate with comfortably. Try to pick a family medicine or sports medicine physician who is pro exercise medicine, an advocate for building healthy bodies through lifestyles adaptations, and practices what they preach.

Cardio-Vascular Exercise

Let's start with a beginning level of cardiovascular exercise. This simple aerobic program includes guidelines for frequency, intensity, and duration.

Frequency:

- 3-5 times per week
- Start with three days and work up to five days per week

Intensity:

- First, choose your activity. Walking, biking, swimming, aerobic exercise classes, etc.
- Beginning level people should work to a "sweat" level (feel your forehead for light perspiration).
- Start easy and progress to a comfortable level that challenges you and still allows you to talk comfortably (talk test).

If you want to be exact, use the "Karvonen" formula to determine heart range maximum level (HR max). This calculation is a basic formula and uses 220 beats per minute as a normative baseline, minus your age; this number represents your HR max. Then subtract your pulse rate to determine reserve heart rate (RHR). Target heart range is determined by multiplying your RHR by 50% to 85% (preferred work-level) and adding back your pulse rate.

Example: A 50-year-old with a heart rate of 70:

- 220 (-) 50 = 170 HR max, 170 (-) 70 = 100 RHR (Using 60% as your work level then adding back your pulse rate) 100 RHR (X) .60 = 60 + 70 RHR= 130 target range.

*Remember, this is an introductory program and is just a guide. Also, I know that this can get confusing, so don't be afraid to ask qualified personnel for help to clarify or adjust.

Duration:

- There is considerable debate about how long to do cardio, and I am sticking to the established general guidelines of working up to a minimum of 15 minutes per session.
- Increase your total daily exercise time each week by 10% to 15% until you reach approximately 30 minutes per session.

Explanation:

- If you're doing 15 minutes per day, three times a week, that equals 45 minutes of total exercise per week.
- In the following week, increase total weekly exercise by 10%. For example, 45 minutes x 10% increase equals 4.5 min increase in a daily session.
- This increase then results in 16.5 minutes sessions and 49.5 minutes per week.
- Continue increasing weekly by 10/15% until you reach your goal of 30-60-minute sessions, 3-5 times per week.

Total Body Fitness

Total body general fitness is also an integral part of a heart disease prevention plan. Everyone should consider adding these critical components of fitness.

- Muscle strength
- Muscle endurance
- Flexibility
- Balance
- Maintaining normal body fat (under 30 BMI)

The above fitness areas should be categorized and added to a weekly program. We know that this could be time-consuming, so we recommend adding some components to the warm-up and cool-down phases. These components greatly enhance heart disease prevention and should be done at least 3-5 times per week.

Currently, 150 minutes of weekly exercise is recommended and has become somewhat of an activity norm. Unfortunately, only a fraction (under 10%) of this nation's population exercises regularly at this level. We understand that two and a half hours of activity sounds like a lot to the non-exercising world, but many exercise specialists, including us, believe that's the bare minimum.

Also, people concerned with aging deficits must find a way to include consistent movement patterns and training, routinely, into their life, for life. Activity for life is a cardinal principle and an axiom of this book. Too many individuals are intermittent and seasonal trainers. These short-term exercisers have overwhelmingly poor results, and their unrealistic expectations doom these people to failure. Reaching good health and fitness goals requires a long-term commitment.

While getting started can be challenging, and the preliminary stages can cause some undue stress, people who persevere begin to realize that they are experiencing a noticeable change for the better in their lives. People feel self-satisfaction about making those positive changes and soon realize that there's nothing better than feeling healthy and good about yourself.

Healthy Lifestyle = Healthy Heart = Healthy Life

Super-Aging does not recommend dieting; we endorse healthy eating and believe it represents inhibitory medicine. Food programs like the Mediterranean, Mind, and Dash are dietary recommendations that emphasize whole grains, nuts, fruits, vegetables, and legumes (beans, peas, pulses) as their baseline. These eating formulas have many similarities, but there are subtle differences between these plans in fish, poultry, red meat, and unrefined cereal consumption. Still, overall, they are all balanced and have a good track record for success internationally. The point is that these nutritional guidelines are not short-term weight loss fixes; they're long-term healthy eating strategies.

Don't be seduced by the latest revolutionary fad or exotic food regimes. Overall, these diets are terrible for your health. Lowered immunity and increased susceptibility to disease are common. Additionally, quick weight loss diets result in reduced muscle and increased fat. On top of all that, your metabolism takes a beating! Binge dieters, almost always, are doomed to fail! If you're feeling lost on nutrition, seeking out a qualified nutritionist or dietician is a great place to start.

Our last cardio prevention key closely parallels heart-smart exercise and healthy eating. Unhealthy poundage has quickly become an epidemic, and controlling your BMI is a significant key to heart disease prevention. Experiencing an excessive body mass gain that is not related to exercise and training can be very concerning. Small girth gains happen to everyone, but substantial short-term weight and fat increases (over 10%) can be disastrous.

Never get to the point where you need extreme measures. Rebounding and going back to an average weight is as tough as it gets. If you maintain a consistent exercise program and eat a healthy diet, reaching and maintaining a sturdy and lean body is much more likely.

The biggest takeaway from this conversation is that heart disease is generally a long-term, gradual, step by step, progressive, and developmental lifestyle disease. However, individuals can curtail this dangerous trend at any time or stage! It is the world's greatest killer, yet incredibly, it's often controllable.

In Summary:

- Start a comprehensive cardio astute exercise program. Consistently maintaining your exercise routine helps control blood pressure, promote lean body mass, and reduce the incidence of diabetes.
- Maintain a balanced diet and lead an active life.
- Combine all the above with not smoking, controlling depression, reducing stress, and eliminating other addictive behavior. Then, unsurprisingly, heart disease becomes controllable and much less likely to occur. On top of all that good stuff, you'll look better, feel better, and have more energy.

Cancer

Cancer is life's ultimate demon. Many people believe that cancer control is somewhat unattainable. But, contrary to old beliefs, some cancer incidents can be lessened or controlled with lifestyle modifications and early treatment.

Don't Smoke or Stop Smoking

Refraining from smoking, or quitting smoking, also tops the list for reducing cancer risk. We have already discussed the threat that smoking and tobacco products have on premature deaths in CVD cases. According to the U.S. Department of Health and Human Services, cigarette smoking is responsible for more than 480,000 deaths per year in the United States, including more than 41,000 deaths resulting from secondhand smoke exposure.

In their October 28, 2020, newsletter, the American Cancer Society reported that smoking causes about 20% of all cancers and 30% of all cancer deaths in the United States. Despite significant declines in smoking in the U.S., it still accounts for most lung cancer deaths. About 80% of lung cancer deaths are due to smoking. Lung cancer is the leading cause of cancer death in men and women.

On top of those dismal statistics, smoking also increases the risk for other cancers. Here's the shortlist: mouth, larynx, pharynx, kidney, cervix, liver, bladder, pancreas, stomach, colon, and rectum. Let's be unequivocally clear and concise on our stance regarding inhaling any type of tobacco; there is no safe way or method. Despite significant declines in smoking in the U.S., it still accounts for most lung cancer deaths.

Maintain A Healthy Weight

Next, the unhealthy weight epidemic is a primary risk factor for premature cancer deaths, and many researchers are now reporting that excess weight is the second biggest cause of cancer. We know this is a troublesome subject to discuss, but not having this conversation potentiates disease-causing factors, including cancer, and grossly affects people's health. Here are just a couple of examples.

Dr. Farhad Islami's critical findings on October 3, 2017, the Morbidity and Mortality Weekly report published by the CDC included these findings. Of all cancers, fifty-five percent in women and twenty-four percent in men were associated with being overweight. The report also suggests that having an unhealthy weight was associated with more than 630,000 cancer cases involving Americans in 2014 and included 13 types of cancers.

On September 5, 2017, News-Review published in Cancer Control Research, Dr. Mitchell Roslin states, "Obesity is going to surpass cigarette smoking as the leading cause of cancer deaths." The take-home message here is that proper nutrition and maintaining an appropriate weight are essential for maintaining healthy living standards. Being grossly overweight is not inert and impacts virtually every aspect of your body, and not in a positive manner."

Physical Activity

Exercise programs have been discussed, so we will not go into too much detail in this section. Remember that Super-Aging Secrets is all about promoting active lifestyles that produce body fat reductions, consequently decreasing cancer risk.

We include a special mention of colon cancer, the second leading cause of cancer deaths in the USA. Many researchers believe that we can reduce bowel cancer risk and decrease many deaths by incorporating daily activity into our lives. According to the NIH Cancer Institute report on physical activity and cancer, in the 2016 meta-analysis of 126 studies, individuals who engaged in the highest level of physical activity had a 19% lower risk of colon cancer than those who were the least physically active.

Despite these reports, patients are not routinely advised to incorporate exercise programs into their daily routines. Our research suggests that regular physical activity can be a valuable treatment option for some colon cancer survivors; therefore, we recommend discussing this with your physician.

Diet and Food Choices

Be aware of poor food choices. Meal quantities, quality, and the preparative ingredients may cause reactive or incomplete food absorption. In other words, your body doesn't like the junk food you're putting in it! CRAP is a descriptive acronym many nutritionists use to represent carbonated, refined, artificial, and processed foods. It's hard to believe, but these poor food choices are far more prevalent and pronounced in today's indulgent world. Therefore, we add an "E" representing embellish to punctuate and form the new word, CRAP(E). Hopefully, that word turns you off enough to make you think about what you're eating.

We feel it's important to warn people of the preponderance of food additives now used to produce these savored mixtures. Just the calories added to these foods should make you highly suspicious of what you're putting into your body. We know this simple fact from dealing with well-known chefs that they believe, and rightfully so, most people are not overly excited to eat foods that don't taste good. These restaurateurs understand that consumers want tasty foods, so they find ways to make their foods more desirable by adding flavorful additives (sugars, syrups, fats, oils, salts, colors, etc.). Beware!

Like Pavlov's dog (a Russian physiologist known for classical conditioning), we all salivate just thinking about these sumptuous dishes. Foods like loaded nachos, greasy pizza, mac and cheese, deep-fried foods, cheesecakes, and cream pies are just a few of the many examples. Unfortunately, these food choices have become somewhat standard for many Americans but certainly aren't the best choices for your health.

That doesn't mean you can't eat certain foods; it simply means over-indulging in addictive foods may have long-term effects on energy production, dense tissue formation, and growth. In addition, compulsively eating junk food adds unhealthy fat accumulation in and around vital organs and muscle cells. We believe that natural, organic, chemical-free, high fiber, and CRAP(E)-free food choices will enhance life and decrease cancer risk.

As we age, we gain fat lose muscle and bone density resulting in increased adiposity, lower energy, decreased metabolism, and increased cancer risk. Eating less but eating better becomes more vital as we age. Lean meats or protein alternatives, ample calcium, and fiber should be considered to promote muscle and bone maintenance and decrease fat. The result is reduced cancer incidence.

Other Probable Common Risk Factors to Watch Out For

- Genetic predisposition
- Excessive sun or UV light
- Uncontrolled alcohol consumption
- Over inhalation of air pollutants
- Varied contact with chemical components
- Hormones such as estrogen, progesterone, testosterone may be linked to breast, ovarian, endometrial, and prostate cancer genesis.
- Microwave and electrical exposure
- X-rays
- Viruses and infections
- Occupational hazards
- Medical treatments
- Etc., etc., etc., the list continues to grow.

At this point, it seems like everything and anything can cause cancer under certain conditions. Suffice it to say that scientists and researchers worldwide pursue cancer causes and cures.

I would be remiss if I didn't mention the tremendous distress of facing a possible cancer diagnosis. We compassionately understand the enormous apprehension that a cancer diagnosis brings, but many of these cancers are not necessarily life-threatening. Spontaneous reactions should not be based on fear. Weigh your options carefully before choosing overly aggressive and frequently overzealous approaches.

Examples of aggressive treatments include surgeries, radiation, and chemotherapy. Less invasive choices like stem cells, targeted therapies, bone marrow, immunotherapy, and hormones are becoming more mainstream and are often viable alternatives. Numerous other conservative care treatment options are also being developed and are beneficial for special populations. Rushing to choose aggressive treatment for non-imminent cancers is not always in your best interest. We will explain further later in this section.

Treatable Cancers:

Skin and prostate cancer are two relevant examples of mostly treatable early conditions. These disorders are usually low-risk and non-life-threatening. First, let's discuss prostate cancer, the most diagnosed cancer in men. Frequently men choose aggressive treatment, including surgery and radiation, due to nervousness and anxiety. Are these decisions wise or reactive? What are the alternatives, and are they appropriate?

Prostate Cancer

Although prostate cancer is the number two cause of cancer deaths in men, it's such a slow-growing problem that most men will die from something else before they die from the prostate issue. The American Cancer Society reports the five-year survival rate for localized cancer (no sign of cancer outside of prostate) is almost 100%.

These numbers and SEER (Surveillance, Epidemiology, End, Results) score are based on men diagnosed with prostate cancer between 2010 and 2016.

Seer Stage 5-year Survival Rate:

- Localized: Nearly 100%
- Regional: Nearly 100%
- Distant: 30%
- All SEER Stages combined: 98%

Skin Cancer

Our second example is skin cancer. In most cases, these growths are also non-life-threatening. People have become highly fearful of the sun and, conjointly, outdoor activity. The National Cancer Institute reports that skin cancer is the most widely diagnosed cancer in the United States.

Basal and squamous cell carcinomas are the most common skin cancers in the US. Let's repeat this vital reality, these non-melanoma skin cancers can usually be cured and are mostly non-life-threatening. Overreactions to these conditions can do more harm than good. Discuss this with your physician and seek out alternative opinions if in doubt.

In June 2021, the American Academy of Dermatology website reported that melanoma skin cancer is more likely to spread to nearby tissues, making it harder to cure. Most skin cancer deaths are from melanoma. In 2021, it was estimated that 7,180 deaths would be attributed to melanoma—4,600 men and 2,580 women.

Undoubtedly, one death is too many, but understand that 7,180 deaths are a relatively small number when you consider approximately 5 million skin cancer cases diagnosed per year in the US. Even the more deadly melanoma cases are highly treatable with high survival rates. Weigh your options carefully.

Another critical issue is the viability of reading and evaluating skin biopsies. A report published by MedlinePlus on June 29, 2017, stated that individual pathologist reports, when assessing skin biopsies, could vary significantly for melanoma, especially when the case is not clear-cut. This study demonstrates how important it is to consider a follow-up biopsy to verify a positive skin cancer test result.

Our only suggestion is to educate yourself about treatment options when possible. We know how complicated people's decisions are when facing a cancer diagnosis. Accordingly, our only recommendation is not to panic. Do your homework and discuss your cancer issue with numerous practitioners. Hopefully, you can include trusted family members and close friends you feel comfortable with when talking about your cancer situation.

Educating yourself will help you base your decision on an informed and researched conclusion. Having confidence that you've made the right decision will go a long way in winning the fight against this dreaded disease.

In Summary

This last section is of paramount importance to cancer survivors.

We understand that beating cancer is excellent news and should be celebrated, but your quality of life can often be in jeopardy. We hate being the bearer of bad news, but cancer survivors should know that treatments often result in premature aging, prolonged health problems, and shorter life spans. Chemotherapy, radiation, and other cancer treatments are associated with numerous long-term issues, including frailty, nerve damage, hearing loss, muscle weakness, arthritis, immunity problems, impaired healing, dementia, and more.

The good news is that the post-cancer side effects can often be alleviated by promoting appropriate activity and exercise. Remember, Super-Aging Secrets is all about maintaining living skills for life. So, preventing further breakdown and restoring lost skills and deficits on a case-by-case basis, whenever possible, should still be a primary goal. Many researchers report that brisk physical activity is linked to better survival rates. Cancer survivors almost always have something in common: inner strength and resiliency.

We don't pretend to understand how complicated life can be for cancer survivors, but we still believe that being resolute is imperative. Live life to the fullest, with the greatest gift being that you can maintain your active and independent lifestyle whenever possible, for most if not all your lifetime.

**As a side note, we want to be clear and definitive regarding intimate medical care decisions. Our only goal in this book is to educate and inform on treatment options. We do not advise on cancer choices and respect all individual decisions regarding prospective cancer treatment.

Respiratory Diseases

First, what does respiratory disease mean? Recently, medical professionals have categorized progressive lung diseases into an associated bundle. Chronic Obstructive Pulmonary Disease (COPD) disorders mainly involve constriction of the airway and labored breathing. This umbrella term primarily includes emphysema, chronic bronchitis, refractory asthma (non-reversible), etc. Other respiratory diseases are also included but are beyond the scope of our presentation. Primarily we are talking about blocked airways leading to breathing problems.

Symptoms include:

1. Shortness of breath and wheezing
2. Chest tightness
3. Sputum: coughing up phlegm that changes colors
4. Chronic cough
5. Headaches
6. Trouble sleeping
7. Extreme fatigue
8. Blue lips and nails
9. Regular flare-ups of above-stated symptoms.

COPD

Although COPD includes chronic asthma, the two most common and destructive respiratory conditions are emphysema and chronic bronchitis. The basic definition of bronchitis is inflammation of bronchial tubes leading to airway swelling that produces excess mucus. In other words, the airways leading into the lungs become constricted, causing fluid retention, resulting in insufficient oxygen transfer. Emphysema takes it to the next step and involves the alveoli (air sacs, which resemble grapes on a vine) of the lungs becoming damaged and enlarged, causing breathlessness. The damaged and enlarged air sacs cause decreased air exchange resulting in less oxygen inhaled and less CO_2 exhaled into the bloodstream.

Most definitions of COPD include chronicity of symptoms. Chronic bronchitis involves mucus-filled coughs that last at least three months of the year for two years in a row. Lung damage is permanent with progressive and accelerated deterioration in chronic COPD and emphysema. NIH senior health is currently reporting no cure for COPD, but treatments and lifestyle changes can help manage symptoms.

COPD includes refractory asthma, which can be severe and life-threatening but usually favorable. "Asthma may be fairly easily controlled and even reversed with medications," notes Dr. Len Horovitz, in a study published by Lancet Respiratory Medicine in August 2017. Asthma deaths are also rising, with as many as 40,000 deaths reported annually worldwide. "

On September 29, 2017, Health Day News stated that the number of Americans who die from chronic respiratory diseases has skyrocketed over the past 35 years, primarily led by deaths from COPD. They also reported that from 1980 through 2014, more than 4.6 million Americans died from a range of chronic respiratory illnesses. In a second analysis, the University of Washington's researcher Laura Dwyer-Lindgren stated that eighty-five percent of all deaths (3.9 million people) were from COPD, including lung conditions such as emphysema, chronic bronchitis, and to a smaller extent, asthma.

In another research analysis from Respiratory Medicine in 2017, author Theo Vos states that "although these illnesses are primarily controllable or treatable, they have received less attention than other prominent diseases like cardiovascular disease, cancer, and diabetes."

The primary risk factors for these diseases are smoking, air pollutants, allergens like fumes, chemicals, and dust. Non-chronic asthma is more common, but COPD is more deadly. Asthma is usually curable and even reversible, with minimal long-term damage. In contrast, COPD is also treatable, but there may be long-term permanent damage and decline in lung function that can be lifelong.

Solutions

When discussing respiratory syndromes, everyone should be aware of environmental issues. We know that chronic exposure to air pollutants, in many cases, is something many individuals can't avoid. Frequently, many people can't pick where they live but being aware of daily exposure to pollutants and allergens can help you decrease your chances of experiencing life-altering and maybe even life-threatening conditions.

Again, we must mention that stopping cigarette smoking is imperative to reducing respiratory problems. A large percentage of people (ninety percent) with COPD have smoked. Regrettably, even short-term smoking can cause significant lung damage. Still, the good news is that quitting has a regenerative effect on long-term smokers and can reduce or reverse recurring symptoms.

Other solutions revolve around improving health and fitness. Daily activity can decrease severe episodes of life-threatening breathing problems significantly. Super-Aging believes that exercise is not used enough to treat these disorders. However, the importance of physical training is gaining some credibility and is being used more often in the medical world. Hopefully, this trend will continue and become more mainstream.

Our opinion is that patients should explore respiratory specialty exercise programs and protocols with their physicians. We believe that lung expansion exercises, rhythmic breathing, chest stretching, and postural symmetry can improve respiration. Brisk walking and other low to mid-level aerobic programs can be invaluable when treating breathing disorders.

In Summary

- Respiratory problems and diseases develop over many months and years. If you want to avoid irreversible long-term lung damage, it's imperative to address symptoms as early as possible.
- Most people are unaware of how many people die each year from chronic lung diseases (4 million worldwide). Many researchers are now rating COPD, right behind heart disease and cancer, as the third leading cause of premature deaths!
- Although many cases are treatable, sadly, chronic issues continue to cause severely compromised lifestyles.

One of our primary goals is to inform people of high-risk diseases that decrease their chances of remaining active and independent for life. Part of maintaining function is always promoting better air exchange through postural symmetry. Be aware that poor body posture or curvatures can compromise air passage, exacerbating breathing disorders.

Remember that air flowing through straight open tubes (airways) makes air exchange more effortless. Just think about sucking air through a straw that's blocked, curved, or bent! Not easy, right? Head, neck, shoulder, back, and hip positions should align (see Chapter 6), resulting in good air exchange. Postural symmetry isn't discussed enough when talking about the importance of air exchange and breathing disorders. Chapter Six further explores the importance of posture and associated issues.

Stroke

According to the CDC, nearly 800,000 people suffer a stroke each year in the United States. There are also more than 140,000 deaths from strokes annually. If that statistic isn't alarming enough, you could face long-term disability and at least some dependent care if you're fortunate enough to survive a stroke. Understanding the severe long-term effects of stroke should alarm everyone.

Here's what recent reviews are reporting about stroke prevalence. Quan he Yang, a CDC research scientist, states that "80% of strokes are reducible." Research reviewers have also noted some surprising conclusions about strokes that everyone should understand. Ten controllable risk factors accounted for approximately 90% of all strokes worldwide. These statistics are shocking, and we cannot emphasize the importance of re-reporting these findings to the aging population.

Most people know someone who has had a stroke, and understanding that a high number of these strokes can often be averted is invaluable information. If you asked the public, what can you do to control the risk of stroke? Most people would either have no answer or an incomplete answer, so let's talk about the top ten risk factors for stroke and what you can do to decrease your risk for dealing with this ominous issue.

<u>The Top 10 Risk Factors:</u>

1. Hypertension
2. Inactivity
3. Poor Diet
4. Obesity
5. Diabetes
6. Smoking
7. Heart Disease
8. Stress
9. High cholesterol
10. Alcohol misuse

**Note: Hypertension is universally agreed upon as the number one most important factor. Physical inactivity, poor diet, and obesity follow as consensus picks. Numbers 5-10 are interchangeable depending on researchers' preferences.

We again want to emphasize that Super-Aging is about decreasing disease chances and precluding treatment. Let's emphatically state that stroke may be the most clear-cut example of an acute incident that individuals be dramatically reduced. Many researchers, including Dr. Yang (see opening paragraph), have concluded that at least 80% of all strokes can be avoided!

Let's talk about the top risk factors and understand how they cumulatively increase stroke occurrence. Sedentary lifestyles, inactivity, and unhealthy eating consistently lead to weight gain resulting in developmental hypertension, type two diabetes, high cholesterol, and heart disease. The first step to reducing these disease-causing agents is starting an exercise program and incorporating a healthy diet.

Again, don't smoke or quit smoking, and limit alcohol use. Try and lessen stress through lifestyle changes and social interaction whenever possible and, if necessary, get treatment. Reducing these risk factors will limit stroke occurrence. We discuss specific diet and exercise programs later in the book.

Another thing that we need to mention is that most people do better when they discuss their issues, needs, and goals with other people they know and trust (family and friends). We all know uncooperative people and need a little push to get started. You can't help someone who doesn't see a problem or want to help themselves. Many people become conditioned to accept and ignore poor lifestyle choices. Regrettably, it's almost normal today to be in poor health and have a lifestyle that is at high risk for disease development. It's a slippery slope, so watch out!

If you are in poor condition and your health is declining, it's time to have that epiphany and ask yourself if you want to become a burden to your family in your later years. If the choice is no, now is the time to make that lifestyle change that gives you the best chance at living a lifelong independent life.

Catastrophic stroke incidence is about as scary as it gets. One day you're okay, and the following day you experience paralysis of half of your body (hemiplegia), resulting in varying degrees of dysfunction. A nightmare! Besides the high number of deaths, the number of people who become disabled is hugely concerning.

You talk about being afraid of something. A stroke should lead the list of fears in life. The problem is that no one ever thinks it's going to happen to them. The fact is that stroke incidence is way too high, and we need to bring those numbers down. Reducing the incidence of stroke is doable!

In Summary

- If you have symptoms of hypertension, seek evaluation, and get treatment if necessary because this is the single most dangerous risk factor.
- For secondary stroke treatment, reduce fall risk through balance training to prevent further injury.
- Victims of stroke need to understand that long-term treatment and intense rehabilitation (1-3 hours a day for many months and sometimes years) are often necessary to restore essential ADLs (activities of daily living). You need to be all-in on rehabilitation! Do not settle for short-term treatment and think there is nothing else you can do.

In review, closely examine the Top 10 leading risk factors, determine your weaknesses, then start reducing those primary issues. An essential part of lowering the Top 10 risk factors is lifestyle changes starting with maintaining at least 150 minutes per week of exercise. Eat a balanced diet, preserve a healthy weight, get routine physicals, quit, or don't smoke, and control excess alcohol. These steps combine to reduce stress, decrease type 2 diabetes, lower cholesterol, prevent excessive weight gain, and most importantly, REDUCE STROKES!

Unintentional Injury: Accidents, Drugs, and Varied Medical Issues

Unintentional injuries, including accidents, drugs, and medical issues, occur at alarming rates. Motor vehicle accidents have traditionally topped the list of accidental deaths among all age groups, but a new enemy has emerged. Alarming statistics are now being reported about documented drug use and abuse amongst hundreds of thousands of individuals. We report vital statistics later in this chapter. Too many people are experiencing increasing risk and dependency involving opioid medications, debatable prescription drugs, and an untold number of other over-the-counter medicines and supplements.

The National Institute on Drug Abuse reported that in 2019 nearly 50,000 people in the US died from opioid-involved overdoses. In addition, the CDC stated that 841,000 people have passed away from overdoses since 1999. In 2020, the CDC cited the highest number of recorded overdoses ever, 93,000. Sadly, most people believe these early departures are primarily from young, disturbed individuals lost in a world of disharmony and confusion. Unfortunately, that's only part of the story because many of these lost lives were from prescription drugs and included a large percentage of elderly Americans.

It's well documented that opioid abuse is catastrophic. Still, at the same time, most people don't realize the tremendous issues caused by using multiple medications. This type of drug use is simultaneously causing an innumerable amount of side effects and interactions.

The Center for Ethics does systematic reviews of hospital charts. They found even properly prescribed drugs (aside from prescribing error, overdosing, or self-prescribing) cause about 1.9 million hospitalizations yearly. Another 840,000 hospitalized patients are given drugs that cause severe adverse reactions, for a total of 2.74 million serious adverse drug reactions. About 128,000 people die from drugs prescribed to them, and many of these life-threatening events can be reduced.

It's imperative to understand that daily drugs are incompatible with advanced fitness and health. It is extremely tough, maybe impossible, to build a sound body while taking multiple medications. Additionally, chronic drug use produces harmful addictions and compromised lifestyles. Bottom line: if you want to be active for life, consider non-drug measures first whenever possible.

Other notable factors that cause premature deaths are occupational hazards, unsafe homes, and community environments. These predisposing problems in and around you are multifactorial, but being observant and aware of hazardous conditions can help you avoid a potential injury. Complications from surgeries are also becoming a preeminent concern. A good example is a hip fracture. These bone breaks are linked to a much higher risk of death soon after injury and persist for many years to come.

Medical errors have also become a significant concern. In a study published by BMJ in May 2017, Johns Hopkins University researchers analyzed eight years of U.S. data and concluded that more than 250,000 people died each year due to medical errors. Examples include diagnostic errors, monitoring issues, drug-related dose or timing problems, and procedural surgery issues.

Deadly falls have also become common in older adults. Researchers are now warning that one out of every three older adults over 65 will fall at least once a year. Some of these events will lead to serious injury, including deaths. Balance training is now considered an essential part of overall fitness, and most physical medicine specialists have developed courses to help people maintain their equilibrium. Exercise training can be done at home using single and double leg stance routines and associated multi-level movement patterns. Also, rhythmic dance and martial arts classes are excellent for equilibrium. Everyone can reduce fall risk by routinely doing some form of steadiness, proprioceptive agenda. If you have advanced problems, seek a professional specializing in restoring stability.

Accidents come in many forms, but understanding perilous conditions may help avoid a possible catastrophe. As we grow older, our insecurities increase proportionally. Unnecessary risk-taking, addictive behavior, and irrational, compulsive lifestyles are precipitously not good for your well-being. Primary decisions will happen to everyone, so we strongly suggest that you take your time and weigh your options before doing something that could be irreversible and, worse yet, life-threatening.

Unintentional injuries are quickly rising and, if not addressed, will be right up there with heart disease and cancer as a primary precipitator of early deaths. Some researchers are already placing these life threatening-non-intentional episodes (accidents) as our Number 2 killer. The CDC has reported that 39% of unintentional terminal injuries can be avoided! Super-Aging believes that with this growing epidemic of disastrous incidence, the CDC figure could grow much higher in the future.

New information on drug interactions and deaths from medical error also put accidental occurrences as a leading cause of premature mortality. Recapping these astounding numbers; 93,000 drug overdoses, 128,000 fatal interactions of prescription drugs, and 250,000 medical errors resulting in premature deaths each year should be a wake-up call to everyone. Reducing these prospective numbers is a must!

Other unexpected fatal accidents include motor vehicle accidents, poisonings, and falls. Poisoning now leads this infamous list. The National Safety Council (NSA) 2021 reports that poisoning resulted in 65,773 fatalities. Motor vehicle accidents deaths spiked in 2020 to 42,060. And lastly, fall-related deaths concurrently rose thirty percent to 29,668 in 2018, per the CDC. We are now experiencing dramatic increases in all these areas, most likely related to societal impairments, deteriorating lifestyles, and increasing drug and alcohol use and abuse.

Unfortunately, these injuries are challenging to manage and are somewhat spontaneous. How we react to these split-second situations is unteachable for the most part. However, how we lead our lives and good individual judgment can often be protective. On the other hand, poor decisions juxtaposed with irrational behavior can frequently result in many other acute and tragic events. Maybe we shouldn't call it accidental? Choose how you live your life wisely, and remember, safety should constantly be on your mind.

Special Mention

Be on your guard when it comes to averting addictions. No words and no warnings are strong enough messages for addiction. There is no doubt that these behaviors are a leading cause of unintentional injury, trauma, overdose, and premature mortality. Talk about destroying lives! Even if they survive, many addicts never fully recover. Substance misuse disorder has become an epidemic with dire consequences to the addict, family, friends, workplace, and community. Smoking continues to be the number one risk factor for diseases and deaths, but drug and alcohol abuse also compromises millions of lives every year. Self-awareness and control are imperative. Once addicted, life completely changes. Don't wait until it's too late.

The statistics and data are relatively clear and straightforward. Understanding that many sudden accidents and deaths can be substantially decreased is an imperative. Weighing your options carefully, and making mature decisions, might someday save your life!

In Summary:

- Beware of substance use and abuse, including prescription drugs
- Practice medical oversight and judgment
- Keep your guard up while driving
- Avoid unnecessary procedures and surgeries
- Work on maintaining fitness and balance to avoid unnecessary fall risk
- Beware of unsafe conditions in the home and the community
- Be cautious when dealing with occupational hazards

CHAPTER 6: Guaranteed Yet Controllable Aging Issues

We have all heard the old cliché, "Nothing is certain in life except for death and taxes." Unfortunately, there are five other guaranteed physical conditions that everyone will experience during their lifetime if they live long enough. This chapter will list and discuss these predictable and potentially destructive conditions. Every aging adult needs to know that with due diligence, these problems are all reduceable, usually treatable, and often controllable! Lastly, and most importantly, all five of these syndromes, if ignored, can result in life-altering and even life-threatening dilemmas.

What Are These Guaranteed Physical Issues?

1. Sarcopenia (muscle loss)
2. Osteoporosis (bone loss)
3. Orthopedic problems such as (back, knee, shoulder, hip, etc.)
4. Postural changes (spinal, skeletal curvatures, and other asymmetries)
5. Arthritic degeneration (progressive loss of joint cartilage and tissue)

These afflictions are part of a continuum of life. You're born, grow, mature, reverse course, and begin a wearing away process. Like everything else in nature, these eventualities are not predetermined or in any way exact. Like the law of polarity, buildup and breakdown are opposite poles. Finding an equilibrium between these two extremes epitomizes how you age. The point is constant erosion due to aging does not have to be your future, and some development can continue throughout life. Our role in this chapter is to alert everyone to these disease entities and help maturing individuals establish guidelines to deal with these dilemmas.

Consequential Lifelong Issues Defined and Available Options

Sarcopenia

The simple definition of sarcopenia is the progressive loss of muscle mass, muscle strength, and associated decline of physical function with aging.

Every aging person, including the fittest people on the planet, will lose a significant amount of strength as part of the aging process. So, how much muscle motor unit decay will the average person experience? Currently, there isn't any bona fide consensus about the exact degree of muscle wasting over time; however, there is some agreement on the average percentage of strength cells lost periodically during our lifetimes.

Some estimates conclude that we lose approximately five to eight percent of muscle per decade, starting around age forty and increasing to ten to fifteen percent of muscle declines after age seventy. We believe that these estimates are highly conservative and are likely considerably greater. Super-Aging uses basic arithmetic to calculate an approximate average norm. We estimate (.8) percent muscle loss per year from ages forty to seventy years. Simple math then concludes that you'll experience about twenty-four percent muscle loss in thirty years. At that point, chances are this muscle decay will double to two percent a year, depending on your health and fitness levels.

Although we would like to keep things simple, calculating these muscle losses is, at best, confounding. Those muscle-wasting statistics don't essentially tell the whole story. The good news and all-important message here is that healthy lifestyles, sound nutrition, and consistent weekly exercise routines could decrease losses by about fifty percent. That's right, nearly half of all muscle wasting could be preserved or maintained. Wow!

Since this is so monumentally important, let's explain further. We must accept that every person will lose some muscle, and physical recovery will be slower as you age; that's just reality. The optimistic part is that with mental fortitude and perseverance, maintaining a large percentage of old muscle and building new muscle (barring significant injury or disease) can almost always be accomplished in older populations.

Another essential point about sarcopenia is that it is usually defined as a slow and progressive muscle loss. This definition is not always correct and makes it seem like muscle losses are purely a result of the aging process. In other words, you're just old, and muscle loss is simply part of aging. That drip-drip, yearly, and long-term effect of losing muscle make it seem like there's nothing you can do about it, and long-term muscle loss is simply a component of time.

This thought process is far from the truth. Unfortunate incidents like sickness, injury, trauma, surgery, disease, or other chronic or acute disorders can expeditiously cause significant muscle declines. The truth is that any illness or harmful event that results in long-term rest or immobilization can cause lifetime losses of muscle strength and mass. Understand that even short-term bed rest (less than seven days) can account for double-digit losses of muscle strength.

Anyone who works with the post-injury, post-surgery population sees muscle atrophy routinely. Early training teaches therapists to measure these anatomical areas bilaterally as a guideline for rehabilitating these injuries/surgeries. For example, what happens when comparing the regular patient's uninjured side with the surgical site after ACL knee reconstruction? This procedure can cause as much as two to three inches of quadricep tissue losses in the ordinary person. Restoring this massive loss becomes a demanding challenge, and the average person seldom fully restores these deficits. Even with highly motivated upper-level athletes, tissue regeneration, if accomplished, still takes approximately 12-24 months.

John Hopkins Medicine cited a great example in a 2014 news release: ICU patients can experience three to eleven percent muscle loss per day with intensive care treatment. Although this is not a typical example and involves life and death, it epitomizes the possibilities. Think about this astonishing and inconceivable finding on metabolic soft tissue losses. In only one day, you can lose up to 11% of your muscle. This type of data is a message to all individuals on how fast we can deteriorate in extreme situations. Caution is advised!

We cite this data to inform and educate aging individuals who voluntarily choose rest and immobilization as primary treatment. The message is rest and immobilization also have long-term consequences. Muscle mass is intimately tied to our metabolism. Losing muscle can have a cascading effect on many areas of one's health and fitness, including:

a. Increased risk of developing other metabolic diseases such as high blood pressure, diabetes, high triglycerides, high LDL cholesterol, and high central fat
b. Compromised functional capacities that lead to fall risks and gait compensations

c. Other physical skills deficits can result in an inferior quality of life and possible partial or even complete disability

A severe medical issue demands focused and total restorative rehabilitation to counteract extreme muscle wasting. Reducing strength deficits and getting anywhere close to your previous average level may take months and sometimes years! Don't be fooled; losing thirty, forty, and even fifty percent of total muscle is not unusual after a severe medical issue.

Short-term therapy seldom restores overall deficits, especially muscle losses. It's vital to know that all patients should be given a continuing in-home program designed to return them to their pre-injury status when organized therapy is finished. In other words, when scheduled treatment is complete, rehabilitation is not.

Now that you're healed, you should have the tools to continue striving towards complete recovery. The long-term goal is to return to your previous level of function whenever possible. Most importantly, lack of full rehabilitation makes you more prone to future problems, diseases, and long-term muscle issues like sarcopenia.

Sarcopenia is quickly becoming one of the most common problems in the elderly population. According to the National Institute on Aging, there will be 525 million people over sixty-five in 2010. Projections are that by 2050, the senior population will increase to 1.5 billion elders. This populace boom represents a three-fold increase in the 65 plus age group. Because of this fact, our health care system will be heavily taxed if we don't start early restorative rehabilitation for muscle losses in aging individuals.

Insidious, Deceptive, Muscle Changes

Unfortunately, very few people are screened for sarcopenia. Usually, it is not found unless it's associated with other chronic health problems. Unfortunately, muscle strength and mass changes will usually not be picked up in an annual general exam. You'll need to take the initiative and tell your physician about the shortfalls you're experiencing with regular daily activity. In too many cases, people think, "I'm just getting old." Unfortunately, everyone ages, but is aging your actual problem? Did you ever think maybe, just maybe, you're getting weaker?

Some troubling concerns to look out for include:

- The inability to climb stairs or rise from a deep-seated position
- The failure to get up after lying on the floor (very concerning)
- Getting in and out of a car becomes a chore
- Going to a restaurant and sitting in a booth or a high-top table is a challenge
- Climbing up to a stadium seat to watch a ball game without help is not only strenuous but also can be somewhat embarrassing
- Shopping or walking on different surfaces begins to be demanding, laborious, and sometimes even an impossible task

Internally you know something is wrong, but you're just not sure what it is. Catch it early because building muscle is relatively straightforward and uncomplicated in the beginning stages! These budding situations are in many ways warning signs of growing weakness secondary to muscle loss and looming sarcopenia.

In Summary

a. Sarcopenia is a muscle-wasting disease that often causes inefficient and compensated physical function. These changes are almost always associated with slow, gradual, and developmental loss of muscle strength and mass.
b. Sarcopenia is associated with osteoporosis, diabetes, cardiovascular disease, obesity, inflammatory processes, and hormonal change.
c. Aging results in long-term tissue deficits and weakness, but associated physical problems will always follow if muscle loss continues and sarcopenia develops.
d. Progressive resistance exercise, aerobic conditioning, and dietary adjustments have effectively limited muscle losses. Other treatments now being investigated include gene therapy, hormone replacement, and nutritional supplementation.
e. Growing old is a given but losing physical function is not. Do not accept these motor declines as a normal part of aging.
f. If you feel you can't restore your physical capacities and strength on your own, see your doctor and get a referral for physical medicine.

Whenever possible, don't accept medications, bracing, aides (crutches, canes, walkers, etc.) as your primary treatment plan. If insurance doesn't cover you, try finding a senior facility or community center to assist you. Ask family and friends for recommendations. Seeing a good trainer or therapist could be invaluable in helping you restore your ability to lead an everyday active life. Remember, with minimal exceptions; you can get that muscle back regardless of age. Sarcopenia is reducible and, in many cases, reversible!

Osteoporosis (OP): The Bone Thief

Osteoporosis is also referred to as bone thief or silent disease. These verbal connotations accurately describe this devious, deceitful, and degrading loss of bone integrity.

Experiencing an unusual bone fracture is one of the most common symptoms of osteopenia or osteoporosis. Like sarcopenia, OP is usually not diagnosed until someone experiences an unexpected bone break, especially in women over 50. If a second fracture occurs, it becomes likely that you are experiencing bone thinning, and testing will almost always begin.

Finding out that you have bone density issues after a fracture is concerning because, at that point, it has already progressed. Your bones have become decalcified, and treatment for OP is now necessary. Here we go again, another disease that could have been avoidable.

What do you need to know to decrease your chances of developing osteoporosis?

1. What are the risk factors?
2. When do you start your maintenance plan?

Thirty-four million Americans have low bone mass (osteopenia) and are at risk for osteoporosis, according to the NIH Best Exercise Program for Osteoporosis published by DSW fitness in 2014. Below are a few more facts from this study:

- Eight million women and two million men have osteoporosis in the US
- Eighty percent of the people who have OP are women
- Thirty-three percent of men older than seventy-five years of age have OP
- Fifty percent of women a twenty-five percent of men over fifty years old will have an osteoporotic-related fracture in their lifetime

How does osteoporosis develop?

Like sarcopenia, the first thing to remember is that OP happens over months, years, and decades (mainly over decades). OP is not direct, not noticeable, and notoriously unexpected. Somehow this burglar sneaks up on you and steals your inner bone density. Now you have a fracture that demands safeguards and prohibitive measures. Immobilization, casting, rest, and medication are in your probable future.

Could we have diminished the bony changes that lead to fracture? The answer is not conclusive, but it is certainly possible with awareness from you, your family, friends, and medical advisors.

Reducing the incidence of osteoporosis starts relatively early in life. Like muscle girth, bone density peaks around 25-35 years of age. Building dense tissue mass from childhood to adulthood provides a structurally sound base. That's right, building up hard tissue strength is a lifetime proposition. Unfortunately, that doesn't always happen! Don't panic because it's never too late to build adequate skeletal integrity, or at least maintain what you have.

The first step is to start an exercise program or an activity, preferably a weight-bearing activity such as walking, running, dancing, hiking, aerobics class, weight training, golf, racquet sports, martial arts, gardening, etc. If exercise isn't your thing, just stand up and do something in an upright position for a minimum of two or more hours daily.

Next, incorporate a nutritionally sound diet into your life. These two steps alone will help maintain strong, durable bones and give most individuals a good chance at prohibiting osteoporosis.

Yearly physical exams are always recommended but remember; this is a sneaky disease that's easily missed on regular examinations.

What About Getting Bone Scans Routinely?

- Should we get one?
- Do we need one?

Even if you and your doctor decide to do a bone scan, you should know that these tests are not necessarily conclusive and can be misleading. Measuring bone thickness is an imperfect science, and test results are calculated using norms to determine your score. The problem is if you don't know what your bone density was before testing, how are you supposed to know if your score is better, worse, or the same over any given period? Although these tests are not absolute, getting this testing done does have some merit because now you at least have a baseline.

Additionally, bone density scans don't always represent true bone strength. Bone strength is dependent on not only density but also complete mineralization, plus collagen reproduction. The bending property of bone, hence the integrity of bone, is dependent on collagen composition. The percentage of collagen is not measured with typical bone scanning techniques. So, if you're diagnosed with osteopenia or early osteoporosis, this finding may be somewhat misleading and incomplete.

Even if your bone test is within normal ranges or a second follow-up test shows improvement, your bones may still be fragile. As a result, you still can be at high risk for fracture and continuing breakdown since dense bones are not necessarily strong bones. Think of rotted wood; it may look good on the outside and have some pulp on the inside, but you know it's porous and will break easily as soon as you handle it.

We are reviewing this information because our concern is that too many people are not conscious of the long-term changes that occur throughout a lifetime. Getting an exact diagnosis is difficult enough; on top of that, developing an appropriate treatment plan is a challenge and imperfect science. We will discuss this later in this section. Our point is, don't react to this disease. Osteoporosis development can often be controlled if you understand how and why this skeletal decay develops:

Pertinent Traits to Know and Watch For:

Who is at increased risk for developing this silent disease? Like many other syndromes, some people are at a higher risk than others. Those individuals' traits include:

- Being a female is the number one causative factor
- If you're female and happen to be Caucasian, Northern European, or of Asian descent, your risk is more significant, especially for those with a petite frame

- Following menopause, and for five successive years, women are at exceptionally high risk for bone loss of as much as twenty percent.
- If you have a family history of OP, be on high alert because this syndrome often occurs in close relatives.
- An uncommon fracture or numerous fractures after 50 should be investigated, and a follow-up should be scheduled.
- Chronic use of medications (glucocorticoids, anti-seizure drugs, cancer drugs, thyroid hormone are the most common) can be precursors and should be monitored.

If you're in one of these high-risk groups, your chance of developing osteoporosis is greater, and early treatment is the key.

Aging beginning at 50 for women and 70 for men increases developmental OP risk. Age is the number one risk factor, so, unfortunately, you will be more prone to bone loss if you live long enough! The older you get, the higher your chance of osteoporosis, especially in sedentary and deconditioned individuals.

Super-Aging preaches that the first thing necessary to reduce OP is maintaining a healthy lifestyle. You can't deter this disease without leading an active life, and inactivity is by far your leading modifiable risk factor. Super-Aging believes that any type of weight-bearing activity (walking, jogging, racquet, and team sports, dancing, weight training, or just standing and doing things around the house) is an essential component in battling bone loss problems.

Spaceflight research in a microgravity environment is somewhat analogous to people who live sedentary lives. Bones need the pressure to remain dense, and gravity keeps bones strong. Astronauts have been shown to lose more bone mass in one month than postmenopausal women lose in one year. They lose so much bone because there is no gravity, hence no load on their bones. Pressure on bones is what keeps them strong. We need to realize that non-weight-bearing lifestyles (no pressure, no load) will most likely result in gradual bone loss.

An interesting note to comic book aficionados; why was superman so strong? He came from a planet with a red sun which theoretically produced higher gravitational pressure. Hence, the result was high anatomical load, leading to increased body resistance to stress, causing high bone density to resist force, resulting in a super person. No different than here on earth!

Diet is next on the modifiable list. When possible, Super-Aging endorses and believes in getting essential nutrients through a regular, healthy diet and not through supplementation. Women fifty and above should consume around 1000 to 1200 mg/per day of calcium (milk, cheese, dairy, fortified foods), and men should digest 1,000 mg/day when under seventy years old and 1200 mg/day when over seventy.

Vitamin D recommendation is 600 IU/day for fifty-to-seventy-year-old plus groups. The best sources are fifteen to thirty minutes of sunlight several times per week, oily fish, egg yolks, liver, and red meat. Individuals should also add phosphorus and magnesium to their diet. Nuts, seeds, beans, and whole grains are good sources of magnesium. Meats, poultry, fish, and nuts provide ample amounts of phosphorus.

These are general norms and could be found in The Best Exercise Program for Osteoporosis or other manuals on OP supplementation.

Another necessary adaptation is to modify your exercise program to include total body muscle strengthening. A familiar statement is almost always true, strong muscle results in strong tendons and ultimately leads to sturdy bones. This simple statement says it all: if you maintain or improve your muscle mass or tone, you're likely to avoid bone loss.

Reducing secondary risk factors is also essential to discuss. These include:

a. Working on balance to minimize fall risk and fracture potential
b. Maintaining general fitness
c. Being suspicious of unexplained weight loss
d. Prioritizing hip and lower body strength

What about prescription medications? There is no doubt that calcium prescriptions prescribed for high-needs patients are an essential part of the treatment for OP. We do not comment on specific prescription drug use; this topic is outside our scope and reserved for discussion between you and your physician.

Also, be aware that prescription drug supplementation only, especially calcium, has been and continues to be the most frequent, unilaterally prescribed OP treatment by many doctors. Let's clarify.

Prescription drug supplementation has often been used without joint resistive movements and weight-bearing programs. In reviewing the literature, we believe that including exercises in treating osteoporosis is a more comprehensive and credible approach in most cases. If treatment becomes necessary, we recommend discussing the addition of exercise training approaches to your program with your physician.

Our opinion is in complete agreement and corroborated by BMJ's Too Much Medicine Campaign published in May 2018: We paraphrase, drug treatment can achieve a marginal reduction in hip fractures at the cost of unnecessary harm and a considerable waste of monetary resources. Evidence on the cost-effectiveness of drug treatment is entirely lacking, and this focus on drug treatment means that those feasible alternative strategies, such as physical activity, are overlooked.

The steps to take in decreasing your risk for osteoporosis are:

1. Don't allow yourself to become inactive.
2. Make sure you are getting adequate calcium and vitamin D.
3. Don't smoke or stop smoking.
4. Work to maintain total body muscle strength and mass.
5. Incorporate lifetime exercise, especially weight-bearing movement.
6. Add balance training to your program to reduce fall risk.
7. Beware of unexplained weight reduction; this may be a precursor to early bone loss.
8. Know when you're losing your ability to execute daily activities because this is a sign of growing dependence (sit to stand, stairs, poor gait pattern, etc.). Do something about it before it's too late! Remember, strong muscles equal strong bones.
9. Be aware that you could experience structural and bone alignment changes if you lose bone integrity. These bony changes frequently lead to curvatures and can be permanent.
10. Monitor people (50+ women, 70+ men) who are chronic users of medications.

In contrast to sarcopenia, visually identifying possible early warning signs of osteoporosis is somewhat objective. Many people with significant bone loss will exhibit observational qualities that can be picked up with a physical exam. Examples are abundant: advancing age, postmenopausal women, lean frame, body wasting, low or poor muscle tone, loss of height, thoracic curvatures (kyphosis), and point tender bones are just a few of the prominent signs that can be observed.

So, when should treatment start for this silent predator? Most observers agree that postmenopausal women can lose 20% of bone density for the next five years after beginning menopause. This tremendous loss alone should be enough for females over fifty to start an exercise program that helps build or preserve bone.

Optimistically speaking, we recommend women start programs before menopause begins, but if that doesn't happen, then definitely soon after menopause. We believe men should also initiate programs in the early stages, preferably in their fifties or sixties. These bone preservations programs are effective and safe with almost no side effects.

With consistency and perseverance, the reduction of osteoporosis can be accomplished. Don't wait until it's too late because weak bones are susceptible to structural breakdowns. Treating these conditions after they develop is, at best, an insurmountable challenge. Don't wait for those fractures, don't wait for painful spinal changes, don't wait for that catastrophic fall, don't wait until it's too late! Start your program today.

Postural Changes

Although postural changes are noticeable and evident in the aging population, there's not an abundance of investigators researching this consequential subject. We believe this topic is of substantial importance to all age groups, most notably middle-aged and above. The older population should be acutely aware of bony compensations resulting in a structural breakdown. Does an aging person have to experience progressive body asymmetry? Not only do these misalignments cause pain and dysfunction, but they also potentiate growing medical conditions and pathologies.

Let's talk about the skeletal deformations that inordinately occur in the aging population. What are the repercussions of these changes?

Everyone knows an older man or woman that has gradually gone from an upright posture to misalignment to an altered unbalanced appearance. Before they know it, they're walking around curved, bent over, and looking at the ground. Instead of having an abnormal upright appearance, they're now a crooked person who's considerably shorter. What happened?

Typical examples are a forward head, shrugged or protracted shoulders, hunched or deviated back, elevated rotated pelvis, long curved bones (femur, tibia), bowed or knocked knee(s), flattened arches, and twisted toes.

Over time, the elderly experience some loss of height because of decreased spinal hydration and degenerative changes, causing verticality to be challenged. Super-Aging believes that some of these postural problems are reversible, adjustable, and manageable, but others are regrettably permanent! You've seen it; they often become considerably smaller and rounder.

Let's talk about the upper body first. Deviated head positions are significant when evaluating posture, and a forward head is probably the most common deviation. If uncorrected, it will eventually lead to other structural changes. Typically, shoulders will rise and protract (move forward), causing scapular-thoracic elevation resulting in a kyphotic (rounded, hunched back) posture.

If this isn't bad enough, respiration will be compromised, affecting normal breathing and oxygen exchange. Head up with shoulders back is still a mainstay in maintaining optimal posture, resulting in better aesthetics and better symmetry, improved respiration, and more efficient movement.

The trunk and lower body deformities are commonplace and become more widespread as we age. A familiar deformity is forward anterior pelvic tilt leading to lumbar lordosis and abdominal bulging (beer belly). The result, if not corrected, is total body adaptations and eventual loss of normal curvatures.

Progressively the spine becomes curved, rounded, or both. We move towards a more fetal position. Instead of having linear aligned anatomy (ear, shoulder, hip, knee, ankle forming a straight line), we regress to forward head, protracted shoulders, flexed trunk, bent knees, and contorted frame. This positional change is highly inefficient, and walking becomes strenuous.

One of the essential things the body must do is absorb shock. The inability for any joint to absorb or transfer force will eventually lead to gait compensations, fatigue, balance issues, and fall risk problems. Imagine an older adult using a walker. You'll see arms bent with head and body over the walker, trunk flexed, knees bent, and struggling to push the walker forward.

As a result of this positional change, everything these individuals try to do in an upright position becomes difficult. These gradual changes (often irreversible) don't always have to happen. Maintaining postural alignment and symmetry is an ongoing battle in aging individuals.

Your body's bony alignment and structural integrity are imperative. It affects nerve conductivity, pressure gradients, oxygen exchange, muscular strength and endurance, skeletal density, soft tissue elasticity, body equilibrium, and joint stability. These functions are all dependent on:

- Body's positional balance and counterbalance
- Controlled muscular contractions
- Reciprocal co-contractions
- Synchronous guiding and steering mechanisms

I know this gets a little complicated, but it's essential to understand that nothing in your body works well when it's twisted or contorted. This anatomical change leads to compromised and constricted pathways, altered functions, and inefficient movements.

These deviated patterns then lead to an overload of other linked body sections. In other words, another soft tissue area or joint commonly breaks down, most likely, on the opposite side. If a further breakdown happens, your active life is truly in jeopardy.

I don't want to sound like your parents, but they were right. Don't slouch! Keep your head up, pull your shoulders back, maintain your spinal alignment, and don't let your hips and knees remain flexed. If you can do this, life will be much better for you, especially if you want to maintain an active lifestyle. These compensated patterns almost always cause reactive fatigue, overload, and injury issues making movement more demanding.

Counteracting curvatures is one of the many reasons that postural awareness and training should be a part of everyone's weekly routine. The aging population should focus more on body stabilization exercises vs. traditional prime muscle group training. Muscular imbalance and contracture contribute to postural asymmetry.

Rhythmic breathing, scapular efficiency, spinal stabilizations, range of motion, and flexibility, coupled with total body extension programs, should be included as a part of postural integrity and alignment programs. As we get older, muscles that control (scapular, spine, core, pelvic, hip, etc.) are more critical than larger muscle groups like the pecs, lats, biceps, triceps, quads, etc.

Visualize a tree. You don't want the branches on the tree to be bigger than the trunk of the tree. Don't get me wrong; there's nothing wrong with working what I call the "pretty muscles," but if you want to stand tall for life, it's better to address the small control muscles. I can't emphasize enough the importance of maintaining good posture through a balanced exercise approach.

Also, be aware that postural changes can occur with developing sarcopenia or osteoporosis. Weak muscles and hollowed bones are far more malleable (bendable), causing them to reshape. These issues often compound and progress into a postural catastrophe waiting to happen. Alignment changes are now inevitable!

Understand this, if bone curves or bends, you're not bending it back. Skeletal changes resulting in deviated curvatures are untreatable for the most part. Some surgeries can be attempted, but the long-term results of these procedures are highly speculative and questionable. Do your homework before attempting.

Like Sarcopenia and Osteoporosis, these slow long-term changes are seldom picked up until they have already developed. A routine physical exam rarely includes total body posture, so it's best to self-monitor when you can. Here are a few simple things you can do:

1. Try observing body alignment (head position, shoulder height) in a mirror.
2. If you stand against a wall or lay on your back, feel if all body parts touch the wall or ground.
3. Full-length mirrors are great for observing pelvic, hip, and leg positions.
4. Self-monitoring will help alert you if things start to change.

Many times, painful areas are the result of growing structural deformation. Back, neck, and spinal pain are the most common. All joints can and do change when stressed, overloaded, injured, and a product of compensations. Hopefully, these changes can be identified by you or a trained person.

Knowing that you have a postural issue should sound the bell in your head saying, let's do something about it! Find a good therapist or trainer who can guide you by prescribing a program of therapeutic exercises. This program should help reduce or maybe even control postural long-term permanent change.

Orthopedic Problems

Out of all the creeping, insidious causes of growing disabilities that we have discussed so far, having an orthopedic issue is the guarantee of all guarantees. We're talking about the hundreds of possible disorders involving the musculoskeletal system. These injuries will happen and do happen to every person, with no exceptions! The great majority of individuals will experience many of these orthopedic problems throughout their lifetime.

Orthopedics primarily consists of bones, muscles, associated nerves, joints, ligaments, tendons, and related anatomical tissues. How you handle these injuries will, in many instances, determine your long-term movement proficiency. As a result of orthopedic problems, will you continue to be active, or will you eventually drop out of sports, exercise classes, health, fitness, or leisure time activities? Will these impairments result in a chronic problem? How often have you heard someone say, "I've been dealing with this problem for months, years, decades, etc."

Even if you recover from orthopedic problems, you may develop issues later in life due to re-injury, scarring problems, miscellaneous general breakdowns, and associated decline. Currently, orthopedic problems are the number one most prevalent problem in the elderly. These issues typically start acutely, move to a chronic state, then, over time, become degenerative. Because of this progression, these issues compound into looming lifetime predicaments. The result is that chronic orthopedic dilemmas, if not adequately treated, gradually affect a person's ability to participate in physical activity and possibly even regular everyday tasks.

Major causes are:

a. Accidents or general trauma
b. Degeneration or wearing down
c. Disuse, or in contrast, overuse
d. Sprains and strains

On top of the above factors, many other people believe wearing away is the primary reason for growing orthopedic problems in the aging population. Is that true? Do you wear out or rust out? Here's a customary statement from inactive people: "I worked hard, I played hard, I overdid it when I was young," and so forth. Their problem is not because of an injury, not because of a trauma, only because they were once active?

These individuals religiously believe in the wear and tear theory of aging (see Chapter 2). The thought process is they've worn themselves out and overdid it early in life, and now they're suffering the consequences. Or some believe that lifelong active or sporty individuals suffer a higher incidence of injury and breakdown as they age. Are they right?

Countering that argument is the now well-accepted realization that inactivity increases orthopedic impairment. The truth is that active people consistently do better at maintaining their quality of life and have fewer prominent breakdowns than sedentary people. Don't be fooled; implementing movement through recreation, exercise, sport, and leisure time pursuits is grossly beneficial for maintaining a vibrant lifestyle.

Now let's talk about seeing your doctor. I know it's diplomatic to say, "If you're starting an exercise program, see your doctor first." Is that true? It's undoubtedly case-specific whether to take that advice. If you have or suspect a primary medical condition and feel your doctor must clear you, seeing your physician makes good sense and is a logical, independent choice. If you're not in any distress, consulting a physician on exercise options is not always necessary.

We hope to alert people that starting an exercise program is now accepted medicine and seldomly contraindicated without disease or specific injury. Let's restate one of our primary messages and a vital statistic; inactivity is now considered a top risk factor for developing injury and disease. Not starting an exercise program may be dangerous to your health!

Don't let orthopedic issues stop you from being active. These problems will happen to everyone, and recovery is the key to staying involved. Restoring lost function through continuing therapeutic exercise programs for life is a must if you want to resume activity for life. Remember another vital Super-Aging Secret. Always reduce, maintain, and restore physical and mental capacities forever. We will discuss this further in upcoming chapters. Now let's examine some of the noteworthy orthopedic dilemmas you will likely face.

Topping the list of all orthopedic problems is back pain. Researchers state that about 80% of the population will experience a back issue sometime in their lifetime. Muscles, tendons, bones, ligaments, and joints of the knee, shoulder, hip, and neck areas are next in line when it comes to injury. These ailments are a universal phenomenon in humankind. Suffice it to say that virtually everyone will deal with not one but many significant bony and soft tissue issues throughout their lifetimes.

Is there a relationship between these injuries and your ability to continue to lead an active life? The answer to the question is an absolute YES! Many people use rest as their treatment plan. Sometimes that's fine but understand that even minor injuries can result in appreciable losses of physical ability, and meaningful injuries can result in gross dysfunction and possible lifetime impediments. If your primary long-term goal is to remain active for life, you must strive to return to your previous activity level or close as possible, with minimum to no restrictions.

Regardless of whether you use formal rehabilitation or do it yourself, your short-term goals should include but are not limited to reducing pain and swelling, having a normal gait, and a minimum of 85-90% of the normal range of motion and strength. Your early focus should be getting back to your regular everyday routine.

After reaching short-term goals, you can progress to general game-related skills, sport-specific programs, and lastly, return to your regular activity or sport. This physical progression is a little slower but has a high success rate. Be aware that even in professional sports, athletes with serious injuries can take as long as six months to one year, sometimes even two years, to return to previous levels of physical skill.

Contrary to the scenario of successful total healing, middle-aged and above individuals typically return to their lives with minimal to no treatment. Remarkably, after a debilitating injury, many patients get no formal rehabilitation, and the great majority of patients get only a few weeks. If you're lucky or have great insurance, you may be covered for a few months.

The point is that you've probably lost considerable amounts of motion, strength, and motor function and don't even know it. Over time, because of your already weakened state, you're just another injury waiting to happen. Understanding this dilemma is what we are trying to emphasize. Don't assume that regular everyday activity is enough to regain your lost function and restore your ability to be active; you must work at it. If you return to your normal lifestyle before you're ready, these cumulative problems will result in growing soreness, pain, associated deficits, and probable re-injury or new injury.

Now, what do you do? You're in pain and having problems in your day-to-day life. Now it makes sense, as a starting point, to see your doctor. Typically, first-line treatment involves evaluation and diagnostic tests. Depending on the results of the tests (if there are no big-time findings), treatment plans will generally start with resting, medication, bracing, possibly injection, and maybe a referral for short-term physical medicine.

If you have a relatively minor problem, these treatments may help resolve your problem, but getting significant relief and restoring your everyday skills is unlikely when dealing with a substantial issue or chronic pain. Unfortunately, more extensive matters will take weeks and months to resolve.

The general healing phase alone takes approximately 4 to 8 weeks and can take considerably longer in the aging population. As reviewed above, restoring an acceptable range of motion, strength, and physical function to pre-injury levels takes time. Don't be fooled into thinking an injection, a brace, medication, and some simple exercise is the ticket to return to normalcy.

Chronic problems frequently occur due to these unrealistic expectations and have become the norm. Millions of Americans who start down that road of unresolved orthopedic injury are now one step closer to growing disability and associated problems as they age.

Along with many orthopedic problems, chronic soreness and pain in mature individuals are commonplace but rarely treated. What is this perpetual soreness, aching, and cramping situation? Is it merely because you're older, or is there another explanation? To help explain this pervasive discomfort and distress, Super-Aging introduces a descriptive acronym called "CARS" (Chronic Age-Related Soreness).

We believe this obnoxious soreness (CARS) is caused by muscle breakdowns due to motor losses, disuse atrophies, joint deteriorations, arthritic decay, chronic swelling, decreased protein synthesis, and growing physical dysfunction. These problems then create pain syndromes and altered mechanics resulting in regular breakdowns. In other words, your muscles and joints cannot handle the stress of everyday life and are in a virtual state of overload, even with a simple daily activity.

Upper body CARS usually are due to contracture, postural deviations, impingements, nerve compression problems, and growing degenerative change. Necks, shoulders, and hands top the list. Improving these issues usually begins with reducing inflammation then restoring your motion. Maintaining neck and shoulder range of motion and stabilizing these areas through scapular thoracic exercise is supremely important. See your therapist for guidelines when necessary

Lower body CARS are more of a concern because they affect a person's ability to be active. Handling your body weight as you age can become demanding. I know it's difficult to put into perspective, but let's give it a try. A normal person in an average day takes approximately one to two thousand steps a day (without exercise). With every step, your body must absorb and transfer your body weight.

Let's take a round number like two-hundred pounds times two-thousand steps (200 X 2000). Doing the math concludes that you must dissipate 400,000 foot-pounds of force each day. Yup, it sounds daunting, doesn't it?

The good news is that an average body can easily handle and transfer this type of force daily if healthy. The bad news is that with growing dysfunction and cumulative muscle and bone deterioration, absorbing regular everyday forces becomes burdensome, challenging, and maybe even impossible for others.

These statements produce safety issues and make everyday life difficult, with growing soreness and pain (CARS). Then the questions that must be asked are:

- How do I solve this constant muscle soreness problem?
- Do I accept muscle aches and pains or just learn to deal with them?
- Do I start working out?
- Do I see my orthopedic doctor and explore medical options?
- Should I try pain medications?
- Do I just stop doing everything?

Hopefully, if you're reading this book, you're probably not the type of person who just gives up when challenged. First, please don't just stop doing things, and stay active by finding alternative things to do (modified activities, cross-train, swim, walk, bike, weight train, etc.) while you search for an answer. Secondly, aging is probably not the only problem; it's not normal to always have ongoing soreness and pain.

Over-the-counter pain medications are acceptable, but we recommend short-term, as-needed use only. Prescription drugs are up to you and your doctor, but we are not big advocates, and we warn that this is a slippery slope. Be advised that if you are not getting relief from physician-ordered treatments, many other alternative medicine treatment options are available. We believe and advocate for Physical medicine and therapeutic exercise programs as the most viable options.

Many professionals in varied movement domains can address specific body exercise programs for seniors, and I would encourage individuals to find programs designed to maintain aging fitness priorities. If you have a particular need, you may have to find a specialist in that area!

Movement and exercise programs are plentiful. Choosing what works for you is paramount. Just one warning, choose activities that you're comfortable doing. If it's something new, make sure you have a knowledgeable trainer that can start you at an appropriate level. Don't burn out, or worse yet, hurt yourself early in the process.

The essential variables are that:

- You enjoy it, which means you'll maintain it.
- Developing a social network around the activity will help.
- Meeting your fitness and rehabilitation goals will be reinforcing.

Remember, keeping your weaknesses strong is a lifetime proposition.

When pursuing lifetime activity, the next thing we must discuss is whether it would be beneficial to see an orthopedic surgeon in the absence of significant trauma or acute disabling issues. Remember that you're seeing a surgical specialist, and it is not a surprise that they believe in surgery. There is no doubt that orthopedists have made tremendous advancements with surgical procedures and are doing excellent work in acute or essential surgeries. But again, let's ask whether it is beneficial to see an orthopedic surgeon in the absence of significant trauma or a disabling condition?

In contrast to imperative surgeries, a growing number of elective and exploratory surgeries are now occurring routinely. The question is, are these procedures necessary or successful for the aging population? Should surgery be your first choice? There's no doubt that some of these surgeries have merit, but other surgeries in the aging population (fifty plus) are either unproductive (minimal to poor results) or unnecessary.

A great example is a partial meniscectomy (knee cartilage surgery):

- John Hopkins researchers have added to mounting evidence that this common surgery in the knee joint brings little or no benefit to people over 65.
- A report published in JAMA Surgery (February 28, 2016) highlights the vast number of avoidable operations performed. "Our study found that this knee operation (knee meniscectomy) is shown to have no benefit in treating degenerative disease, in multiple trials but, is now one of the most common orthopedic procedures in older Americans."

This finding is vitally important to understand! The most common orthopedic surgery (millions of procedures) is shown to have no benefit in treating degenerative knees. The study also states that this specific surgery provides no additional advantage over regular exercise and physical therapy in older patients. These findings are now well accepted, and these procedures have been significantly reduced.

It's also imperative to understand that rehabilitation for a few weeks or even a couple of months is not enough time to determine whether you should proceed with consequential invasive surgery. We preferably recommend rehabilitation for at least three to six months to assess your healing potential. That doesn't mean you have to go to organized therapy for the entire period; doing in-home programs can also be very successful.

Our message is that there are often credible physical medicine alternatives to surgical interventions. There are three probable outcomes here to consider when making your decision.

1. You have nothing to lose but time with this approach (conservative care), and guess what? Many people can get better with long term rehabilitation and avoid other aggressive treatments

2. Secondarily, physical medicine will better prepare you if surgery becomes necessary because you'll be in better condition, and individuals who do pre-habilitation get better surgical results.

3. Thirdly understand there is no worst-case scenario with this type of approach because you don't have to guess; if you get better, you're done; if you don't, you proceed. Use this simple KISS principle to make this critical decision on various treatment options.

Let's summarize this all-important section. Many orthopedic issues will happen to everyone, and reducing your risk involves maintaining your fitness and health. After all injuries, it's imperative to restore losses completely to avoid ongoing problems. See your physician when necessary, and if possible, make rehabilitation your first choice. Staying active for life demands a comprehensive approach to aging dilemmas. We will discuss this further in upcoming chapters.

Arthritic Degeneration: Osteoarthritis (OA)

Arthritis is the final blow of medical guarantees in life if you live long enough. Arthritis is the coup de grace of aging in many ways. In the 17th century France, coup de grace meant "mercy killing" or putting to death a severely injured person who is unlikely to recover. If your perspective is that you want to maintain an active life, this can be the virtual nail in the coffin for many individuals.

In 2021 the CDC reported that 1 in 4 adults in the U.S. is disabled by arthritis. Osteoarthritis is the most common and affects more than 32.5 million people, and many believe it is the leading cause of disability in America! This statistic paints a gloomy picture, but let's not panic just yet because some of these changes are preventable and frequently treatable.

Let's answer these essential questions:

1. What is arthritis?
2. What can we do to prevent or minimize the long-term effects of arthritis?

First, let's define arthritis: Arthron (joint) itis (inflammation) or, plainly put, joint swelling. Other descriptive terms include pain, edema, stiffness, soreness, disease, and degeneration in or around an area where two bones meet (fingers, knee, hip, ankle).

Our definition is the gradual erosion of a joint due to poor healing. Chronic inflammation disrupts the healing process causing gradual decay (breakdown is larger than buildup). The result is the joint continues to erode and never heals completely!

There are two distinct categories of arthritis:

1. Autoimmune
2. Osteoarthritis (OA)

Our focus will be on osteoarthritis (OA). Super-Aging will not get into the various types of autoimmune diseases. These aggressive arthritic diseases (rheumatism, psoriasis, lupus, etc.) are specialized, often severe, and outside our area of concentration. Our only recommendation is to recognize that utilizing physical medicine specialists and timely rehabilitation is essential when managing rheumatological conditions.

In contrast, our position on OA is like aging; it is not a disease; it's a process. A person's ability to withstand gravity and other frictional components by utilizing therapeutic exercise can often diminish and sometimes even reduce OA development.

As previously discussed, all joints must absorb and transfer force and motion. But remember, people are not like wheels on a car that gradually wear out with use. Our joints are alive and resilient; they grow, regenerate, and reproduce throughout life. Our definition of OA, as mentioned above, is that the joint breakdown is larger than overall healing. We need to alter this situation.

So, the billion-dollar question is, how do we reverse that equation to increase joint healing and less joint breakdown? Is that possible? Most people believe that sooner or later, they'll develop arthritis. Regretfully that statement is true, but our goal in this section is to discuss ways to slow or minimize this progression. Super-Aging is optimistic because new research indicates that OA is not essentially a wear and tear problem. Recent evidence shows that individuals with histories of high activity levels have less deterioration (wear and tear) than the general population.

Bodyweight must be absorbed and transferred with a forward motion, as discussed earlier. With walking, you disperse about 90% of your body weight, running three times body weight, and jumping up to five times (or more) body weight. This shock-absorbing system sounds impressive but is the human standard.

Throughout a lifetime, everyone's body will dissipate, absorb, and transfer trillions of foot-pounds of force up and down the body. Maintaining your ability to process these forces, at your level, throughout your life not only protects your musculoskeletal system but can also build it up. Alternatively, grossly losing that ability breaks the body down.

Medical professionals also need to recognize that activity is not usually the precipitating factor in OA and, if they concur, discuss this new information with their patients. Many researchers are now convinced that OA is not primarily a wear and tear disease, and we completely agree! The facts are that if wear and tear were the most significant factors in OA, inactive people would have less osteoarthritis than active people; they don't.

The next question is, what is wearing down in our joints? Everyone has heard the term "bone on bone." When we speak about surface deterioration, we refer to narrowing a joint space between two articulating bone surfaces (the place where two bones meet).

These bone surfaces have padding (articular cartilage) on the exterior of the bone and cushioning between bone surfaces called meniscal cartilage. An example is the knee is composed of the upper bone (femur), meeting the lower bone (tibia). Simply put, when these bones get closer to each other, you are experiencing joint deterioration. The most common areas for OA are the spine, hips, knees, hands, and feet, and less common spots are the shoulders, sacral-iliac (pelvic), ankle, and jaw.

Every aging person will experience some degree of osteoarthritis. Many investigators state that the percentage of elders with arthritis is grossly underreported. Remember, these statistics are only based on patients' diagnoses by a doctor. How many more aren't seeing physicians or don't have symptoms? The Arthritis Foundation reports that for those over 65, more than one in two men may have arthritis, and two in three women may have arthritis.

We believe that virtually *every senior* will have some generalized arthritis and a degree of decay, guaranteed, in some or many joints. These erosions are essentially part of the aging process and are overwhelmingly the norm. You are incredibly blessed and an exception to all rules if you don't. Knowing virtually everyone has some wearing away issues, what triggers problems and eventual treatment?

There are many individuals who experience joint pain, decide to see their physician, and invariably end up with a diagnosis of arthritis. When your x-rays are read, the findings will frequently show some arthritic change, especially in the 65 plus group. Seeing joint space narrowing along with different degrees of spurring, sclerosis (overgrowth, hardening of tissue), and osteophytes (small, tiny chips) is exceedingly common in older persons and easy to recognize, resulting in a diagnosis of arthritis.

Okay, so you have arthritis, now what? Most people then think to themselves and ask, or should ask, what is the treatment? Or is there a treatment? Can arthritic problems be successfully treated? We will discuss this in more detail later in this section. Also, arthritis may not be your only problem or possibly not even your primary problem; there may be other contributing factors.

If you feel comfortable having a conversation with your doctor, ask if other possible issues. If your doctor thinks that there is no need to evaluate further, you have a choice to make. Either accept the diagnosis, get another opinion, or respectfully request a referral for a physical therapy evaluation.

We believe that often other additional soft tissue abnormalities coexist with arthritis. When these other problems are addressed and resolved (swelling, tendonitis, sprain, strain, alignment, contracture, hip, ankle, or foot problems, etc.), the arthritic pain also decreases.

Unfortunately, too many physicians and therapists assume that arthritis is the problem and don't assess other injury possibilities. This assumption leads the patient to believe that there is no natural cure for arthritis and minimal options. Since arthritis is the primary diagnosis, people end up with incomplete treatments such as injections, medications, braces, etc. These procedures have some merit, but they're usually nothing more than short-term fixes and long-term failures. People don't think to try other treatments because they are told that there is nothing they can do. Is that true?

Many studies are now documenting that physical activity, including walking, dancing, yoga, martial arts, aerobic classes, mild running, movement, and other as tolerated sports, can decrease pain and slow the rate of joint deterioration. Invariably, some people will ask, how can I do these exercises if I suffer from soreness and pain? All I can say is start slowly and progress if or when you can. Modify activity if you must. You'll often find out that low-grade movements will improve your problem and sometimes even solve your issue. If not, seek specialized treatment.

In the recent past (last few decades), and even today, some medical practitioners thought, and many still believe, that OA is relatively untreatable. New research now reports that physical medicine and weight-bearing activity are viable treatments for OA and will preserve the joint for many additional years. Even people with severe arthritis, who are candidates for knee replacement, are improving enough with therapy that they can put off joint replacement for the foreseeable future.

Unquestionably, OA is a primary contributor to the loss of physical function. Whatever damage has been done to a joint, in many ways, is irreversible. Unfortunately, as previously stated, this conclusion leads too many people to think that the joint can't or won't heal, and there is nothing they can do about it. On top of that, some physicians tell patients that there is no treatment.

It's undeniable that most people will have arthritis, and it's essentially not going away. Based on decades of experience, our position is that many individuals will recover, persevere, and be active and functional without any advanced invasive treatment. Every joint will heel somehow, someway. It may not be pristine or flawless, but the surface area will frequently scar in and subsequently become or remain functional. Our bodies, when nurtured, are amazing machines that have tremendous healing ability, even in older populations.

So, what are the leading causes of OA., and what can we do to slow its development? The most often cited mechanism for developing OA. is an unhealthy weight. The risk of OA is about 4-5 times greater in individuals with a BMI over 30 making it the number one risk factor for joint disease.

Arthritic processes can also be accelerated by mechanical factors such as joint alignment, spinal curvatures, hip rotations, pelvic obliquity, angular bones, short or long legs, foot deformities, and other frictional deformations. If not treated early, all these structural issues can cause arthritic change.

Premature back, hip, knee, shoulder, and neck surgeries have multiplied at an alarming rate. Having numerous surgeries is extremely risky! If you want a guarantee of joint decay, you got one! Early in life surgeries almost always lead to early in life degeneration and arthritis. Preserve what you can when you can. Losing joint tissue is like losing a tooth. You're not getting it back!

This situation leads us to one of the most asked questions from the aging population. How do I know if it's the right time to consider joint replacement surgery? Regrettably, idealistic thinking has made body parts expendable, aided by evolving technology. Hips and knees were the first to be replaced, now shoulders, thumbs, hallux (big toe), ankles, wrist, fingers, etc., replacements are becoming commonplace. These procedures are significant surgeries involving extensive repair and tremendous tissue damage. Adequate recovery and return to activity are certainly not guaranteed, and our goal of remaining active for life is now in jeopardy.

Everyone should understand that there often are alternatives to some surgeries. We will explain later in this section. I know that everyone wants to believe that they will have a fantastic surgical result, and we wish that for everyone also, but the reality is that older people often have less than optimal results. Unfortunately, you cannot redo an unsuccessful surgery.

Also, we want to make it abundantly clear that we are not against joint replacements; many produce positive results allowing individuals a much better quality of life. Our point is that it's imperative to understand that there can be many side effects and problems.

Here are a couple of studies documenting some of the long-term problems after joint replacement procedures.

- A study published in the journal of Arthritis and Rheumatism (April 4, 2013) and cites 202 study participants states, "Not all patients benefit equally from hip or knee replacement. Only half of the participants reported a meaningful improvement in their overall hip disability and knee pain one and two years after surgery."
- According to the study authors, nearly 83% of study participants who undergo a single joint replacement will have another joint replacement within two years.

**These are just a couple of examples of established procedures that are considered "normal." Our message is to weigh your options because there can also be numerous post-surgical problems. Here are a few examples:*

- Infections, anesthesia issues, and blood clotting can be life-threatening.
- Rehabilitation is often painful, strenuous, and debilitating.
- Scar tissue formations can lead to manipulation procedures (breaking up scar tissue under anesthesia.

- Revisions (redoing the surgery) are more common than people think.
- Not only is there a high risk of never returning to pre-injury levels, but there is also an equally high level of people who go on to have another problem area (compensatory issue), creating the need for more surgeries.

As stated above, many people with joint replacement end up having other surgeries resulting in a reduced quality of life. Super-Aging's advice is to try rehabilitation first. Therapeutic exercise is underutilized and quickly becomes the best option for restoring and maintaining a active lifestyle. Don't be fooled into thinking that you can't do anything to resolve your orthopedic arthritic issue. Overall, rehabilitation should always be your first choice, barring severe or extreme cases.

There is no question in our minds that exaggerated joint replacement expectations have led to many premature surgeries. Many individuals believe this is their best chance of returning to their previous activity level. Unfortunately, getting back to a normal active lifestyle is not guaranteed. And please realize, even if you get a great result but are relatively young (under 60) and live an average lifespan, you'll probably have to redo the surgery in the future.

We believe that there are three fundamental reasons to have replacement surgery.

1. Intractable major pain
2. The inability to do daily activities with growing dysfunction
3. All other reasons are personal so be aware of the possible consequences.

Everyone should understand that in some cases, arthritic problems can be relieved. Don't believe that your only hope is either just put up with the pain or get a significant surgical procedure. Instead, make therapeutic exercise and training part of your life, and your chance for pain relief is better than average with nothing to lose but time. Many researchers and professional observers are now saying if motion exercises were drugs, everyone should get this prescription. We completely agree!

If other treatments don't work and you decide to have a joint replacement, be prepared to work your butt off to get back to somewhere close to normal. Rehabilitation is a long-term proposition (six months to two years) to restore lost abilities and avoid future problems and more surgery. Joint replacement is not a panacea. For some, these procedures can be active life enhancers and for others, activity enders. Super-Aging Secrets' primary goal is to give individuals the best chance at remaining functional and operational for life so will say this again, take your rehabilitation seriously and understand that getting back to normal will take many months and sometimes years. Rehabilitation on that joint continues for life!

In this section on arthritic change, our goal was to alert everyone that rehabilitation and therapeutic exercise can be a viable alternative to many OA sufferers. Executing lots of stress-free motion (weight-bearing and non-weight-bearing) coupled with flexibility and strategic strengthening significantly improves these so-called untreatable joints.

Conclusion

The guaranteed aging issues in life are formidable! Anyone who wants to maintain an active independent lifestyle will be constantly challenged. Most people will face variable, nagging, and never-ending breakdowns resulting in chronic body aches and pains (CARS). If not addressed, these issues will eventually result in the development of injury and disease mechanisms. The outcome is frequently a compromised lifestyle.

Sarcopenia, osteoporosis, postural deviations, orthopedic injuries, and arthritic joint degeneration are all dominant players in the game of life. In some ways, the guaranteed aging issues are somewhat analogous, compounding, and can ultimately accelerate each other. There is no such thing as one problem or one injury. There is probably a dominant issue, but sequential breakdowns cascade into simultaneous matters almost always.

In Summary:

- Address every issue consistently and never let one problem go unresolved.
- Always concentrate on the primary problem first!
- If you're going to remain active, you must know your body and understand what it takes to maintain and prevent another injury.
- Stay active, stay fit, reduce losses, and maintain essential skills for life.
- Rest is relative and sometimes necessary, but remember, the longer you rest, the more vital tissue you lose, and the longer it takes to recover.

CHAPTER 7: The F.I.G.H.T. For Your Active Life

The Five Intrepid Components

1. Faith & Fortitude: Belief plus strength creates a powerful force.
2. Illness & Injury: Always restore losses to prevent future problems.
3. Growth & Genes: Know your genes and never stop growing.
4. Health & Habits: Maintain health through management of habits.
5. Training & Transition: Reduce aging deficits and control your weaknesses.

Introduction

Is your greater fear of dying or becoming disabled? The answer may sound obvious, but losing independence, not death, has become the more feared and onerous option today. Living a long life without good health is not an enviable position. When folks are asked if they want to live into their 90's or even 100's many people respond, Heck No! Who wants to grow old, sick, and frail, then die alone and miserable?

Many aging philosophers refer to this aging fear as the Tithonus effect. According to Greek mythology, Eos (goddess of the dawn) fell in love with Tithonus (a mortal prince). She loved him so much that she asked Zeus to grant him eternal life but mistakenly forgot to ask for eternal youth. The result was Tithonus grew older and older but never died, eventually becoming decrepit. After seeing him in this state of complete enfeeblement, Eos turned him into a cicada, hoping that death would soon come for him. The sad conclusion is, having eternal life without being granted lasting health is more of a curse than a gift.

Many people believe that dying younger and not suffering through aging declines and poor health is better than leading a long miserable life. Does this presupposed aging reality have to happen? The answer is not always. Super-Agers have proven that they can lead a long, healthy, and satisfying existence forever, barring a catastrophic health occurrence, by formulating an individual plan to assist them in navigating life's constant attacks on vitality.

First, let's discuss the different terms and meanings of the length of time lived. Let's clarify the distinctions between total lifespan, healthy lifespan, and healthy functional lifespan. An entire lifespan simply denotes the number of years you live, and a healthy lifespan means years lived primarily free from illness. Lastly, a healthy and active lifespan (top honors) includes good lifetime health, no severe chronic conditions, and simultaneously sustaining everyday activities.

I know it is a high bar, but we advocate a firm determination not to change your basic routine or, at the very minimum, take complete care of yourself for life whenever possible.

There is no shortage of opinions on what it takes to extend your liveliness, spirit, love of life, and juvenescence. Looking and feeling young has been an admired attribute since the dawn of time. Who doesn't look at an elderly but stately person who exhibits a youthful appearance and wonders with admiration, how do they do it? What's their secret?

Here are a few examples of the more common anti-aging treatments available. Cosmetic procedures (surgeries), Botox injections, deep skin treatments, and countless other therapeutics have become mainstream for preserving a rejuvenated appearance. Results can ultimately range from miraculous to mediocre, to miserable, a real leap of faith! I can't conclusively say that these procedures don't work, but caution is strongly advised. Please understand that these beautiful body approaches invariably have many risks and side effects and rarely improve long-term health.

While looking good often translates to feeling good, don't be fooled by what is often a short-term improvement to your appearance. Reality still dictates that you must consistently preserve your health and fitness. Maybe human engineers will someday build or grow you a new body, but there are no shortcuts currently. Maintaining a Super-Aging lifestyle takes commitment.

This chapter lays out an evolving foundation for life. It's not set in stone, and it's not intractable. Instead, it's a working plan with long-term objectives that should be individualized depending on your traits and needs. These objectives should be relatively static but conversely are designed to be flexible and ever-changing as we age, if necessary. These guidelines were created to help individuals understand that growing older doesn't mean catastrophic decline.

The Components of Fight for Your Active Life

1. Faith and Fortitude

Faith

We have partially discussed the incredible power of the mind. This transcendental capacity to will a given mind-body response is truly a phenomenon. As a result, observant and insightful people have grown to understand that you can accomplish remarkable things if you believe. Let's discuss.

Amazingly, positive thinking in the aging population surpasses logical and realistic conclusions. Remember this old meaningful cliché, "light and hope always beat darkness and despair." This heavenly power (positivity) refers to your ability to believe that you can deter obstacles even when the odds are against you. In other words, if you have faith, your chances of overcoming adverse circumstances increase monumentally.

For example, consider a recent article published by Kaiser Health News in May 2018 titled *Believing Stereotypes About Aging Creates Self-Fulfilling Prophecy*.

Author Judith Graham explains, "if you have pessimistic expectations about aging changes, you'll regularly end up with negative results, creating a self-fulfilling prophecy. Consequently, health often suffers." Studies show that adults with negative expectations tend to slowly ambulate, experience memory problems, and recover less fully from a fall or fracture, along with other undesirable consequences. In contrast, those who view aging as primarily positive generally have more vigor, recuperate better, and amazingly live 7.5 years longer than others.

Here's another illogical but well-accepted conclusion, often cited in aging literature. Subjective health status invariably relates to one's ability to maintain independent lifestyles. In other words, if you genuinely think you're doing well, even if you're not, it often results in some progress, even improvement. I can't say it enough, Believe!

Fortitude

Fortitude is defined as courage when experiencing pain and adversity. Common synonyms include bravery, toughness, strong-mindedness, resilience, backbone, spine, spirit, nerve, and my three favorite qualities: patience, perseverance, and consistency. Having fortitude is a tremendous asset when dealing with trying times.

Invariably, everyone will experience some pain and adversity with aging. However, defeating challenging medical conditions becomes a complex and daunting task without fortitude. After forty-plus years working with people on their physical health, I can confidently report to all concerned parties that when people don't give an all-out effort towards full recovery, the results are consistently mediocre, at best.

I will tell you unequivocally that recovering from a complex medical incident in life can become overwhelming. Not having intractable fortitude plus attitude commonly causes poor progression and incomplete results. Remember, our goal is not only to recover but to ultimately restore your active lifestyle and reinforce your ongoing independence.

Having faith and fortitude doesn't always guarantee good fortunes, but, undoubtedly, it is a powerful asset to anyone with these steadfast productive qualities.

2. Illness and Injury

Growing older automatically puts you in the category of high risk and is considered, by many gerontologists, to be the number one risk factor in life. This thought process creates the perception that your issue is merely an aging problem; you're just old. Regrettably, there is some truth to this statement, but be aware of the undeniable fact (minus extreme cases) that there is a tremendous capacity to improve regardless of age.

Many physicians automatically treat aging individuals differently because they believe mature adults are unable or incapable of maximum improvement. We feel this is arguably a misguided philosophy. Aging assumptions are made constantly, and restricted treatments are routinely ordered. Is this always appropriate? Should older people be treated differently?

Barring calamitous or dire situations, we believe that everyone should be working towards complete recovery, even in advanced age groups. That's right, full recovery. It may not always be feasible, but the goal should always be to get back to pre-injury status.

Unfortunately, many practitioners will treat aging people grossly differently. Common misperceptions and skewed beliefs for the aging include:

- You're older, so there's no need to push it
- Because of your age, you should prioritize rest, immobilize the injury, and take medication
- Aging individuals don't need to be concerned about weakness or gait changes
- And getting back to activity is not essential for mature adults.

Too many health care providers are overly cautious and fearful when treating aging people. Excessively conservative approaches involving long-term rest, immobilization, and medications can sometimes cause more harm than good. Under normal circumstances, treatment for older individuals should be like all other age groups. Let's explain.

Illness and injury are virtual lifetime nemeses that everyone will eventually face. Unfortunately, recovering from breakdowns can change as we age due to progressive loss of vital tissue. It is expected that older individuals' ability to heal, restore, and rehabilitate can be somewhat compromised, but that doesn't mean they can't get back to normal. You may have to work a little harder and maybe a little longer, but you can recover.

Reality dictates that we all will face constant and consistent challenges throughout our lives. How we deal with these illnesses and injuries is vitally important. Every medical issue, especially a severe one, has a significant bearing on how you function throughout the later years of your life.

How you deal with consequential medical mishaps (see Chapter 6) has increased importance as we age, making a full recovery more critical. Sadly, one specific medical injury, especially in older age groups, could lead to ongoing issues and problems with your quality of life. One of my favorite statements that I often repeated to my patients was *the number one cause of injury today, by far, and nothing close is poor or incomplete rehabilitation from a previous injury.*

I found out early in my career that many impairments weren't just incidental; they were developmental. Don't set yourself up for future problems by not completing your rehabilitation. After medical release, if you're not back to normal, or at least close to normal, you're just another injury waiting to happen! Now, there's an increased possibility of reinjury, compounding risk, more treatment, and loss of vital skills because of earlier unresolved problems.

Ask yourself: *Do you want to get back to your previous lifestyle?*

If your answer is yes to this question, regardless of age, the next step is to commit yourself to do whatever is necessary to restore normal function. Super-Aging has no reservation in saying you can't rest your way back to normal, especially if you're trying to get back to a previous level of above-average, moderate, or even general everyday activity.

A great majority of the aging population sooner or later will need treatment for a notable dysfunction. If that happens, be aware of insurmountable bony and soft tissue losses (See chapter 6 sarcopenia section) that can occur during long-term recovery from a severe issue (more than four weeks) or even short-term (2 to 4 weeks).

A few weeks of immobilization or bed rest can result in as much as 20 to 40% (or higher) of total body muscle loss. Mature individuals (40 plus) will seldom regain this muscle and face increasing difficulties with their extracurriculars. These poor recoveries lead to problems with full weight-bearing, regular walking, and maybe even routine daily activities like dressing, grooming, restroom duties, and sleeping. Here are a few excellent theoretical examples that help us illustrate the consequences of poor recovery.

In the Disrepair-Accumulation theory (see Chapter 2), Wang et al. suggest that aging results from the accumulation of "mis-repair." The critical point is that when the healing process is incomplete, it accumulates and gradually causes cell disruption, resulting in an actual source of aging. This theory coincides with Super-Aging's hypothesis that incomplete rehabilitation contributes to susceptibility to chronic problems.

Thomas Reid said, "a chain is no stronger than its weakest link." Orthopedic problems are notoriously tied to the growing deficiency of the biological chain (weak links), leading to the inability to transfer and absorb force. Secondary flawed patterns gradually overload the system, and this erratic pattern will almost always result in more breakdown and growing dysfunction.

In *Metabolic Features and Regulation of the Healing Cycle*, Robert Naviaux makes these vital points about incomplete healing:

- Healing is a dynamic circle that starts with injury and ends with recovery.
- Everything in the body attempts to heal somehow, someway.
- If the body cannot complete the healing process, reinjury frequently occurs, creating a vicious ongoing cycle of incomplete healing and reinjury.
- If this cycle isn't broken, ongoing problems persist.

Naviaux believes that this repeating loop is the root of every chronic illness, injury, and recurrent medical issue.

Super-Aging believes the same is true of growing bodily dysfunctions associated with incomplete healing cycles, disrepair, and poor recovery. These disorders typically occur secondary to lack of treatment, inadequate treatment, and most importantly, incomplete rehabilitation. Remember, your goal after significant illness or injury is to return to pre-injury status whenever possible, and anything less sets you up for recurring future problems.

Don't be tentative, don't be shy, tell your doctor that you want to go to rehabilitation to complete the therapeutic process. After discharge from physical medicine, ask for a post-therapy independent in-home rehabilitation program to assure total recovery. Don't set yourself up for future issues!

3. Genes and Growing

Genes

When discussing genes, you need to have a basic understanding of what genes are. A basic definition is the fundamental and distinctive characteristics or qualities, often regarded as unchangeable. Or, put simply, a unit of heredity which is transferred from a parent to a child. In other words, your parents pass along certain traits. Appearance is the most notable, but health may be the most important.

There are about 25,000 genes with billions of DNA letters (pairs). These numbers are incomprehensible to almost everyone and not crucial to our discussion. What is important is what happens to DNA as we age.

Cells are constantly dividing and passing on genetic information. Thus, cell replication is an ever-growing process that allows us to repair ourselves and fix ongoing harm done by the environment and physical mechanisms.

The problem becomes, as we age, some harm is not repaired and stays in our DNA. Consequently, the damage done to compromised cells causes this genetic code to be subjected to severe alteration. This impairment in your family's heredity spontaneously changes gene expression and can invariably be passed on to the next generation. Therefore, knowing your family's gene traits is not absolute but can often help you understand your predispositions and possible future.

How often have you heard someone say, *I woke up one day and realized I became my father/mother?* It's not just appearance; it's physical, mental, and many times, psychological. It's astonishing how similar some families are.

Combining your lifetime health status with your family's history, general testing, and a current hands-on physical assessment is indispensable when assessing your future risk. It's not perfect, but correlating all tests together will give you the most accurate perspective about future and current risk profiles.

Premature aging can often result from cellular mutation, and many other variables can also distort your genetic composition because genes transform and reconstruct. *Having a prolific family history is a plus, but the lifestyle choices make a much more significant impact as you age.* Even if everyone in your family lived well beyond average lifespans, all bets are off in this new era of modern-day degenerative conditions, lack of fitness, and poor health. Let's just say: There Are No Guarantees in Life!!

Growing

What does cellular growth have to do with Super-Aging? The keyword here is GROWTH. Senescence is a term used for aging cells that gradually become dormant, losing their ability to reproduce. They still work, signal, and interact with other cells, but they become unproductive, inefficient, and sluggish. That sounds like the definition of aging! There is no question that this internal process triggers the body to break down. As a result of this cellular stagnation, we lose the working capacities of many metabolizing cells.

Many older people have told me they thought that they were losing strength. They didn't know how or when, but they could sense it. Anyone concerned with aging declines should understand that aging is associated with gradual and progressive loss of essential tissue. You can formulate a plan to reduce some of these tissue losses before they occur if you know, or suspect, this is happening.

If cellular senescence and apoptosis (cell death) continue or accelerate, it raises the risk for ongoing breakdowns. These breakdowns then lead to disease, decay, and dysfunction. Unfortunately, there appears to be no credible way to mediate, stop, or reverse this cellular aging process at this point in our history. The questions then become:

- What can we do to slow down the loss of vital tissue?
- Can we influence or enhance tissue maintenance or development?
- Can we control damage and reduce degeneration?

Our cells are constantly replicating, regenerating, and restoring themselves. For the most part, cells take a daily beating resulting in weakness, fatigue, and eventual failure, and this breakdown then triggers cell rebirth and reproduction. Cells continue to replicate daily, weekly, monthly, yearly, and generationally to keep our bodies from breaking down.

Of course, not all systems are the same. Some miraculously reproduce in days and weeks, many in months, some in years, and others never reproduce at all. The question then becomes, what can we do to protect and even grow vital muscle, bone, and nerve as we age? This growth would allow us to remain more productive, active, and independent for extended periods, maybe even for life.

Now that we understand that growth is an integral part of life, we should maintain as much essential tissue as possible through cellular reproduction. We will repeat this one all-important message in this section since tissue and bone loss are thoroughly covered in Chapter 6. The muscular system and bony skeleton are highly regenerative systems. Muscle and bone loss, when recognized, can almost always be treated and restored in aging individuals.

Nerve regeneration is much trickier. Commonly, the aging population is losing nerve motor units and are predisposed to inhibition (muscle is not working or dormant). Nerve and muscle inhibition often occurs due to disuse atrophy and damage caused by trauma and surgery.

Short-term results are not promising when trying to reactivate an inhibited muscle. Unfortunately, too many people stop trying because of sluggish progress and limited success. Nonetheless, it is possible to restore some of these nerve dysfunctions. It's hard, but some long-term progress can usually be made with perseverance. Hopefully, if you have realistic expectations (months and maybe years) and are patient, you'll get some gradual regeneration.

Remember, our bodies are constantly replacing worn and damaged cells. As we age, this growth gradually becomes slowed (senescent), stopped (apoptosis/death), or accelerated (cancer-causing). Therefore, inactive cell division or genesis (birth) epitomizes and closely parallels aging. Continuing the cell replication, replacement, and repair process determine how you age and how long you remain an average productive person.

You feel it, sense it, and know it, but you can't explain it. You think you're getting old, but what has happened is you've started dying because you stopped growing!

Our advice is to make your journey less turbulent by reducing losses of vital tissue, and you should always promote continued GROWTH! Super-Agers epitomizes the fact that you can revitalize tissue through movement, exercise, diet, and active lifestyles for most of your life and maybe even for your entire life.

4. Health and Good Habits

Maintaining Health

It's almost unbelievable how often we hear about miracle products and treatments which claim enhanced health benefits. Many food sources, drug outlets, and health care organizations promote quality products and treatments, but there are just as many false claims to sift through. It has now become the norm for advertisers (salesmen) to assert that a given product or procedure will enhance your energy, vim, vigor, and of course, good looks. Some of these claims are, to be kind, misleading. Regrettably, most of these assertions fall well short of expectations and are often motivated by economics.

Super-Aging believes that your best defense against acquiring injury or disease is maintaining a balanced and healthy lifestyle. Good health is about preservation, and yes, preservation is treatment! Introducing rapid, quick fix, and frequent change to your body is a recipe for disaster.

Healthy people consistently survive and escape pathologies due to their excellent health and resiliency. Remember the one given trait that Super-Agers have (80 to 100); they don't have a specific major chronic problem or disease. Many people get to an advanced age, not because of extensive treatment but because of a focus on healthy living and having an active and rewarding journey.

Without question, everyone will have to address ongoing health issues, but short-term care is the goal and not long-term treatment. The more treatment you get, the more likely you are to have residual counter effects and reactions. How often have you heard about people being treated for secondary problems (side effects) caused by the initial problems? Frequently these treatments can be counterproductive because they interfere with establishing lifestyle choices that build sound bodies.

The more issues you have, the more your risk factors compound, the worse your health becomes. The numbers are astronomical when looking at cumulative problems arising from primary issues. Secondary care is not always necessary if you focus on complete recovery from immediate treatment. Hopefully, our readers will understand that good health is earned and not bought in a bottle.

Good Habits vs. Bad Habits

Good habits fit right in with good health because you probably have good health if you have good habits. That's a no-brainer, right? Well, not exactly! How often have you heard someone say that someone in their family, a friend, a friend of a friend, a neighbor, an associate, a celebrity, lived a long active life despite all their bad habits and horrible lifestyle? Murphy's laws will tell you that odds are odds, and anything and everything can and does happen. Someone invariably will hit the lottery, while many others will go broke. Is it merely chance, destiny, or choice?

Many individuals believe that some people are lucky, and others are not. If you're one of the individuals who think like this, you might want to rethink your philosophy. I don't understand why some people say *everyone will die from something* or how they rationalize the idea that *when your time comes, it comes, and there is nothing you can do to stop it.* While some people are just unfortunate victims, there is no doubt that people with good patterns, proportionally, have better than average results. It's not luck; it's formulating a plan, making a commitment, doing the hard work, a laser focus, and unyielding dedication.

What about one's odds of becoming disabled or convalescent, i.e., needing complete care? Unfortunately, way too often, individuals with poor habits become dependent and suffer the consequences of their lifestyles. Let's just say that the key to having a productive and rewarding journey starts with reducing or eliminating harmful habits and, in turn, reinforcing good ones.

Now let's discuss other notable bad habits that reduce our ability to lead ordinary day-to-day lives. There is no question that addictions, overeating, and associated sleeping problems are bad habits, but they won't be included in this conversation because they have already been covered in other chapters.

In contrast, inactivity, chronic dieting, and weight control have been reviewed but expanded upon due to added relevance. Other bad habits to discuss are poor food choices, occupational factors, and mental health problems that lead to disease progression and quality of life issues.

Right behind smoking, inactivity is consistently listed as the number two risk factor in life and our number one bad habit. We cover it again because of its importance in preventing the development of other significant risk factors. The Physician and Sports Medicine Journal had it right when they said, "Movement is life. If you stop moving, you stop living". Super-Aging adds that "dead things don't move." Let's be clear, over long periods, inactive lifestyles are consequential and dangerous to your health. There is only one way to maintain your body structure, always keep moving.

Weight control and diet programs have become a big business, so let's touch on the bad habit of never-ending, addictive, and chronic dieting. While there is evidence that calorie restriction can be a reasonable way to reduce weight, compulsive dieting is a bad habit. We understand that many people think it's the right thing to do, but the result of yo-yo dieting is consistently disappointing. Warning, these short-term power diets have not only not worked, but they've caused tremendous harm. Americans are now heavier and less active than at any time in history.

How about food choices? Too many people have become food phobic or lured to eat certain foods. Everyone believes in some fad diet or food trend. What's good, healthy, what is the latest and greatest eating fad? How often have you heard someone say, I'm eating healthy because I eat this (insert fad food)? I don't want to discourage anyone from making good food choices, but our goal is to prevent overeating and encourage balanced diets. See more on diets in Chapter 5.

Work-related problems are highly relevant in our discussion of bad habits. We are now experiencing a new epidemic of perennial problems resulting from jobs that involve mostly sitting, lack of motion, overuse/underuse, or poor working conditions. Employment-related issues are drivers of physical issues and mental health problems. I know it's tough to find a rewarding job but beware of the long-term developmental issues caused by occupational pressures and related anxieties.

Special mention about sit-down jobs. Many researchers now believe that these constant rest positions create destructive health-related issues. Let's start by saying that long-term sitting causes deconditioning. Other frequently reported conditions are muscle degeneration, neck and back pain, compression neuropathies, and links to certain cancers. If you have one of these jobs, you're going to have to spend more time in your off-hours, getting sufficient movement and exercise in your life. Upright workstations are a good solution if you have the option to use them.

Lastly, psychological and sociological issues such as stress attenuation, social isolation (loneliness), depression, poor interactions with family and friends, and lack of participation in community endeavors can potentiate other health-related physical issues. Combining psycho-social issues with physical problems is a recipe for disaster.

In summary, remember this primary yet straightforward point: Reinforcing good habits while simultaneously controlling bad habits is the winning ticket.

In Summary:

- Never stop moving.
- Having a balanced calorie-neutral (burn what you take in) diet promotes lean body mass, reduces heart disease and cancer incidence, and improves mood and energy.
- Lessen the effects of sedentary occupational jobs by finding ways to fit in alternative movement activities whenever possible.
- Control stress and depression through social activity and interaction.

5. Transitions and Training

Transitions

Growing old with grace is a real art. Every individual has their own set of strengths and weaknesses, and it's your job to figure out what yours are. Always maintain strengths, that's a given. More importantly, be aware of any specific long-term deficits because sooner or later, they will potentiate into various breakdowns. Transitions year to year and decade after decade are a must in battling life's timekeeper. As time goes on, your ability to adjust, maintain, and restore these shortcomings will dictate how you lead your life.

I memorized an old idiom many years ago as a young trainer. Don't find out how much is enough by first finding out how much is too much. It's too late! You're already hurt. Aging individuals are at an increased risk for overuse injuries due to inherent weaknesses. Don't ever stop, but at the same time, don't overtrain and don't overuse; consistency is the key to reducing inflammatory issues. Managing your activities and providing adequate rest between high intensity events is vital to maintaining active lifestyles.

How mature adults deal with acute injuries, surgery, or disease is of added importance. We recommend not setting unrealistic expectations after these occurrences. Your priority is always trying to get back to everyday life first. If you accomplish that, you can transition back to a limited return to your activity program at a new modified level. Know your pastimes (hobbies) and break them down into essential components, then drill and practice before you play. Proceed slowly from there with caution.

Knowing how to withstand the rigors of nature will determine if you can continue to maintain normalcy or gradually succumb to the relentless pressure of friction and gravity. Currently, a growing number of aging survivors are proving it can be done. As of 2016, there were 82,000 centenarians (one hundred plus group) in the USA, and researchers predict there may be as many as 589,000 by 2060. Will upcoming generations be able to measure up and maintain Super-Ager standards of living longer and maintaining their lifestyles?

Living life at its most satisfying level is a desirable goal for everyone. However, it's certainly not easy and takes incredible grit and determination. Obstacles are numerous, challenging, and continuous. Your life will change, so you must change. Transitions and lifetime adaptations give you a chance to maintain activity for life.

Remember our motto. "You don't stop playing because you grow old; you grow old because you stop playing" - G.B. Shaw. Don't ever stop participating in life. Get back in the game!

Training

Hopefully, reading this book has helped you understand that aging results in gradual, graded, and progressive loss of vital structural components. What happens when you add losses due to aging with other losses due to injury or disease? The answer is cumulative gross motor losses resulting in growing weakness and physical deficits.

At this point, you may think to yourself; I feel old and weak. Reality is a brutal teacher, but we absolutely recommend you never give in to the thought that you're too old to continue your everyday lifestyle. As we've consistently documented in this book, if you want to be a Super-Ager, you must have the, *yes, I can do it* mentality. You must stay positive! Remember, negative thinkers, overwhelmingly, get negative results.

Activity for life doesn't have to mean you're participating in some form of fitness routine or sport; it may just mean that you're able to get around, shop, dress, work around the house, and interact with others. Participate in something, anything. Try using this old idiom by Edgar Guest that I memorized as a young adult: "I started to sing as I tackled that thing that couldn't be done, and I DID IT!" No better feeling in the world!

Maintain, reduce, restore, rehabilitate, and repeat the process. Continue for life! This Super-Aging axiom is an all-important principle.

If you want to become a Super-Ager, you will need to develop your own specialized therapeutic training routine designed to meet your needs. Everyone has a preferred method for maintaining fitness, and I strongly encourage people to continue participating in their activities of choice. Maybe you're a swimmer, a walker, a biker, a dancer, a weight trainer, a racquet player, a bowler, or a golfer. Or maybe you're just working around the house: gardening, cleaning, shopping, or socializing with family and friends; it doesn't matter.

The important message is that being on your feet and active is imperative. Do something to keep yourself involved with life! It's not the activity that's important; it's your ability to participate at whatever level possible. Training and transition mean adapting to your level of participation.

We try to encourage individuals to stay involved in extracurriculars. The rationale is that participation in a chosen activity will almost always trigger a person to get involved in other associated exercises. If you enjoy biking, you'll probably also do some other form of conditioning so that you can maintain or improve your biking ability, such as yoga or weightlifting.

Another important Super-Aging axiom is to do *your best to evaluate your fitness level, then strive to improve from there*. Maybe you're walking a 25-minute mile; your next goal may be to improve towards a 20-minute mile. I promise, it feels incredible to watch your body improve over time.

Remember this astute statement frequently repeated by many physical medicine specialists, "activity as tolerated." Don't overdue or under-due. Find your comfort level, then strive to move forward from there. Don't give up if it takes more time than you expected; it can be a slow but rewarding process. I know it's challenging to determine fitness levels, but use simple measurements like; activity time, steps taken, weight lifted, heart rate, days of participation, etc.

Organized physical medicine can be beneficial when and if chronic problems have developed. Discuss maintaining or restoring regular routines with your physician, therapist, or trainer. Once released to return to activity from formal treatment, the general rule of thumb is to reduce your previous level of participation by at least 50%. If problems occur, reduce by another 50%. If you're still having issues with the introductory activity, it's time to re-evaluate, cross-train, or reinitiate rehabilitation emphasizing problem areas.

I can't tell you how often I've evaluated people with issues and asked them what their problem is and the plan to overcome it. The point I'm making, again and again, is *if you don't understand what your weaknesses are, eventually, you will fall victim to them*.

Transitions and training are paramount in the game of life, routines must be established, and constant adjustments must be made. This book is about aging and all the pitfalls you encounter daily, weekly, monthly, yearly, and decade after decade. Here are some fitness goals to consider.

- Participate in some form of movement, activity, or exercise session at least 3-5 times per week for approximately 30-60 minutes a day.
- Don't take weeks or months off—there's no time to catch up. You should incorporate year-round activities. Consistency is key!
- Develop a personal secondary plan to work on your specific issues and problems; add to your exercise program, re-evaluate yearly and do it forever.
- Worst case scenario, if you can't move around, just stand on your feet and watch tv, listen to music, do a computer activity, talk on the phone, just be weight-bearing. You'll find out that if you can stand up for a few hours before you know it, you'll be doing other things.

Our health care system might save or extend your life, but it won't restore your ability to live it naturally. Almost all credible health organizations now know that older adults benefit greatly from physical activity. While Super-Aging respects other medical professionals, commonly, the only suggestion people are getting is to walk or exercise in a pool. This suggestion may be a good start since there is no such thing as a detrimental movement, but this likely won't address overall needs. You need to have a comprehensive program.

I like to think of this old lyric by Frank Stanton, "If you strike a thorn or rose, Keep a-going! If it hails, or if it snows, Keep a-going! Taint no use to sit and whine, When the fish isn't on your line; Bait your hook and keep a-trying- Keep a-going'." A little crude, a little old, non-the-less, this is the way to think!

According to the National Institute on Aging, lifespan has gone from 50 years in 1900 to approximately 79.5 years today. Incredibly, there are now more older adults than there are children. There were 524 million people over 65 in 2010, with projected numbers being about 1.5 billion in 2050. Due to these sheer numbers, if aging deficits are not addressed, we will undoubtedly experience an epidemic of age-related problems for decades to come.

Staying independent for life now must be something we don't leave to chance. Progressing through the maze of disease and injury possibilities will separate the people who maintain their lifestyles vs. those who fall into the slippery slope of dependence.

<u>In Summary:</u>

1. Have faith and fortitude, knowing that you can handle all incoming attacks (disease and injury) on your health and fitness.
2. You will not dodge illness and injury, so you must always be prepared to restore lost skills, to get back to your previous level of function.
3. Now that you know you will lose some vital tissue take steps to maintain what you have. Grow! Understand your heredity (family history) so that you can address inherited weak points.
4. Being in good physical condition is your most significant resistance to any injury or disease, which means developing a healthy lifestyle. Double your efforts to reduce bad habits while reinforcing and growing good habits.
5. Lastly, evaluate and re-evaluate your health and fitness level yearly, then transition if necessary. This adaptation means adjusting to your current level of movement and activity. You may move forward, you may move backward, or perhaps you'll stay the same. The point is, re-evaluate your current level, whatever that may be, then move forward from there.

Our message is: You must FIGHT for Your Active Life!

CHAPTER 8: Ways to Reduce, and Control Aging Sequelae

Virtually all aging enthusiasts understand that growing old involves a complicated and intricate progression of unspecified physical, psychological, and social change. We know that all anatomical areas will experience some harmful deterioration. It sounds awful, but the good news is that even late-life potential exists for growth in virtually all bodily systems. The message is that you *must always continue to find ways to maintain your lifestyle and control losses if you're concerned with your quality of life*.

This chapter will discuss the possible consequences of aging, focusing on lifestyle factors that reduce and control the development of disease conditions. Although aging is absolute, Super-Agers withstand these premature aging losses by utilizing distinct characteristics. How do they do it? Now that's the billion-dollar secret that most everyone wants to hear. Let's discuss!

Most people don't realize what they have lost until it's too late. Our aging test outlines definitive age-related changes that must be recognized if adjustments are to be made. Many unknowns and half-truths complicate people's judgment, causing differing views. What's abundantly clear is that not addressing poor lifestyle choices will make you more likely to break down, resulting in premature disease and injury issues. As discussed in chapters five and six, many prevalent conditions and chronic problems are developmental, and their long-term severity can often be alleviated, modified, controlled, or rehabilitated. Educating yourself on these aging dilemmas allows you to formulate a strategy to navigate through the turbulence we call aging.

Some individuals say to themselves *life isn't always fair*. This statement may be somewhat accurate, but maybe a better mindset is thinking that I could bounce back no matter what happens. Physical injuries and disease are part of life, but recovering fully from these problems separates people who persevere and others who go downhill. If disease entities are allowed to incubate, develop, and become chronic, these issues can grow into a declining, degrading, and sometimes even a deplorable standard of living. Our philosophy is: *don't wait for these quality-of-life incidents to happen*.

I don't want to sound like a doomsayer, but why tempt fate? Doing your best to reduce the risk of chronic diseases, frailty, mental diseases, and dependence should be a primary goal for everyone. This potential foreboding future should be enough to convince everyone to do all they can to help avoid sudden injury and disease progression issues from happening to them in the first place.

Today, our medical system is primarily based on reactionary medicine, preemptive testing, and pharmaceutical interventions; these modules dominate so-called protective care today. There is no doubt that controlling disease-causing factors is essential. Still, our goal is to introduce physical medicine plans that make people less prone to contracting a disease or sustaining an injury in the first place? Super-Aging is about inhibitory strategies and building resilient and resistant bodies. As a result, when people get sick, their problems are manageable, short-term recovery is likely, and further treatment is unnecessary.

In our opinion, to forestall injury and disease, you must:

- Have a productive lifestyle:
- Reduce age-related tissue and physical skills decay:
- Use the relevant information learned from aging theories to modify or adjust your philosophy of living:
- Restore functional deficits due to injury and disease mechanisms and simultaneously use Targeted Therapeutic Exercise (TT-E) as a tool to control your specific issues:
- Use Aging facts to help regulate progressive aging!

Five Relevant Discussion Topics:

Topic One: Productive Lifestyles are Integral

Graceful Aging is one of the main messages of this book. Anyone concerned with health should give these two following statements a lot of thought: *You must work for what you want! And, it's much easier to stop something from happening than repair the damage after it has already occurred.* So essential, so elementary, so true.

Super-Agers have lifelong characteristics that define them. They have a higher cognitive function, along with greater oxygen capacity. They also continue to participate in age-related intense physical and mental activity. And best of all, they are relatively free of chronic diseases. These overachievers display physical and mental attributes like individuals 20-40 years younger. Amazing!

Sounds terrific but recognize that these individuals are focused, dedicated and unyielding when preserving their lifestyles. They work at it, impede many things from happening, and are resolute in recovering when problems do occur. Super-Agers are an elite group who are actual survivors, delayers, and escapers of life-altering situations for extended periods.

What is the secret? One of the absolutes when determining the length of active life is, unquestionably, lifestyle choice. There is no exact formula, but engagement in a virtual loop of physical, mental, and interactive social activity is one of the keys to sustaining productive and independent living.

Step Two: Reducing the Long-Term Effects of Aging

This general fitness concept is fundamental but imperative for diminishing or at least controlling *progressive* physical tissue and skill deficits. By participating in cross-sectional exercise programs that incorporate total body fitness areas, you can reduce risk.

- Cardio-Vascular Stamina
- Muscular Strength and Endurance
- Flexibility
- Balance and Gait
- Body Fat Awareness

Unfortunately, everyone will experience a higher incidence of injury and disease as they grow older. This greater rate of occurrence contributes to an increased number of acute, chronic, degenerative, and other incidental bodily breakdowns. Advanced aging occurs when you add regular yearly deficits incurred with seasonal diseases, intermittent acute injuries, and surgeries or procedures. You are now one step closer to life-altering changes. Just like that, you go from active to inactive.

How do we limit these cumulative losses? I know it's challenging, but if you want to remain active, you need to initiate and maintain an ongoing, forever exercise program designed to reduce aging deficits starting with a consistent cardiovascular program (see chapter 5). Regardless of age, muscular power and endurance can be significantly improved in as little as 8-10 weeks of progressive weight training. This all-important fact about restoring strength must be repeatedly stated because the general population doesn't know or believe it!

Flexibility and range of motion should be a part of each program. Most individuals don't understand how to measure their range of motion and flexibility, so I suggest that everyone utilize a therapist or a trainer yearly or bi-yearly (every 1-2 years). This evaluation would be a physical check-up designed to access your muscle and joint-specific motion. Flexibility training would then be based on person-specific issues, implemented, and assigned to be done daily/weekly and invaluable if battling chronic soreness.

The next priority is to preserve balance and gait. The US is experiencing tens of thousands of deaths yearly from falls. Unbelievable! These tragedies can be diminished significantly with balance and gait training. Even elders with considerable problems can improve and sometimes even normalize their gait. Ask your physician for a balance and gait training referral if you can't do it yourself. We'll discuss this in more detail later in this chapter.

Another critical step is to know your BMI (body mass index) and keep it below 30. Being overweight has become an epidemic and continues to grow despite medical warnings. This critical circumstance is not shaming, it is a warning, and it's real! Having excess unhealthy body fat is a valid risk and often limits your ability to remain active. We have already discussed diet so let's just say you should establish and maintain balanced food choices and, most importantly, burn what you ingest.

Understanding and consistently evaluating your cardiovascular endurance, strength, range of motion, flexibility, body fat, balance, and gait will go a long way in limiting aging declines. If you want to maintain an active lifestyle, including activities and sports, you should dedicate yourself to preserving bodily functions, motor skills, and vital tissue.

Always reduce physical losses, then maintain these critical body capacities forever! These vital components are integral in reducing precipitating risk factors responsible for early disease and disability.

Our message is: *keep moving, keep growing and restoring; if you stop trying, you start dying.*

Step Three: Understand Aging Theories and Their Relevance

An abundance of information conclusively documents that living longer lives is intimately tied to lifestyle choices. Hundreds if not thousands of credible researchers and pundits report the wonderous effects of a healthy lifestyle on length of life. I can't emphasize enough how a few adaptations can dramatically improve later-stage living conditions.

Examples

- An NIH study documents Seventh-day Adventist's lifespans; the Adventists' life expectancy is ten years longer, on average, than most Americans. The Adventist's age-enhancing behaviors are regular exercise, a vegetarian diet, healthy weight, and avoiding alcohol and tobacco.
- A Journal of Epidemiology study published in June 2013 involving 6000 men and women, 44-84 years old, concluded that four lifestyle behaviors (regular exercise, a Mediterranean diet, average weight, and not smoking) reduced chances of death by 80% over eight years.
- Pam B. Smith of the Stein Institute reported that three behaviors (exercise, diet, and not smoking) reduced premature death by 57%.

We mention all these studies to highlight that length of life and active lifespan are intimately tied to movement. There is no doubt that what you eat is an essential component but burning those calories has enhanced importance. Exercise and activity are your predominant tool to increase your metabolic rate, preserve lean body mass, reduce obesity, and ultimately lessen aging decay and decline.

To recap, exercise and an active life are critical components for reducing premature aging issues. Sedentary lifestyles and inactivity are quickly becoming the norm, and this lack of movement incubates physical deficits, body mass increases, and early loss of function. Our position is unwavering and is backed up by the above studies and countless other research papers documenting that minimizing the development of these premature diseases and injuries is possible.

The simple message here is that it's clear that with a few adaptations in your daily/weekly routine (exercise, balanced diet, average weight, and no active addictions), your later life can be tremendously enhanced! It's never too late to try; make those changes today!

Step 4: Restoring functional deficits; Introducing Therapeutic Targeted Exercise- (Double TT-e programs)

Our paradigm includes a productive lifestyle, reducing then maintaining bodily tissue and skills diminution, then restoring lost function as the foundation for aging gracefully. Remember this motto; maintain, reduce, restore (vital tissue and physical skills), rehabilitate, and repeat for life.

Restorative exercise is the final cog in our Super-Aging paradigm for graceful aging. It has added importance because significant and compounding physical reductions occur sporadically throughout life. Consistently restoring losses must be an ongoing process and is essential to help avoid chronic problems. This core concept of restorative exercise cannot be complete without addressing the colossal significance of weak links.

Super-Aging now introduces our new concept, Double TT-e programs. Everyone will have a pronounced medical problem, most likely many sporadic breakdowns (chronic, intermittent, occasional) that cause long-term problems with activity. Here are a few examples:

- a restrictive neck or back
- a bad hip or knee
- aching shoulder-elbow-wrist-hand
- a weak ankle
- a sore heel
- foot-feet generalized or specific pain

- numbness, etc.

One problem leads to another problem, and before you know it, you're saying to yourself, *I'm falling apart!* Controlling these weaknesses is imperative if you want to avoid compounding issues.

Recurring problems are by far the toughest to resolve. There will be persistent injuries that never get better as we get older. Double TT-e programs are designed to rehabilitate these long-term conditions and keep those issues from causing other problems. The first step is to assess your situation entirely. Can you answer these simple questions about your chronic issue(s) accurately?

- Has your injury ever been diagnosed? If your answer is yes, what is your diagnosis, and what treatments have you tried to resolve this problem?
- What causes your pain, and what can't you do?
- Do you have full motion and strength?
- Does it swell?
- Is it getting better, is it getting worse? Is it staying the same?
- Do you think it's the same old problem, a new issue, or are you unsure?

If you're not sure, you should find someone who will spend the time to help you figure out what to do. Finding that person is not going to be easy. Start with your doctor, and hopefully, you can get a referral to a physical medicine specialist who focuses on creating individualized home rehabilitation programs.

There is little doubt that your specific chronic problem, if not addressed, will eventually result in more problems and more injuries. Incredulously, most people have already been treated for their injury and failed to restore that condition to normal or close. I've heard it a million times:

- I've always had a bad back!
- My knee or knees have been bothering me for years!
- I've had a bad ankle since I was a kid!

Regretfully, most people have given up on solving that long-term injury issue.

Super-Aging recommends reevaluating your injury issue. As mentioned above, you must identify and understand your problem(s), formulate a plan, and then work on it forever. You need to keep the predominant problem as strong and flexible as possible because if you don't, it will continuously reoccur. Eventually, that same habitual issue will cause elevated pain, dysfunction, and growing disability. Your future now becomes advanced treatment, probable surgery, and a complicated recovery process that can lead to a compromised lifestyle.

In contrast to an advanced procedure, a double TT-e rehabilitation program should be inexpensive (one or two visits), comprehensive, person-specific, and involve minimal or no special equipment. The only thing necessary is a motivated and dedicated person. There are no real negatives to trying this because the worst-case scenario is you'll be more robust, more flexible, and be in better health. Even if your issue doesn't get better, you are now better prepared to deal with other possible treatments.

Special mention to those exercise warriors who think they can just push past these injuries, I admire your gut, but it's unlikely you can beat your injury into submission. Just because you're physically active or work out frequently doesn't mean you are helping yourself. I know many frustrated athletes who think that if they work harder and harder on their fitness, they'll eventually solve their problems. Not likely!

If you continue down that road of heavy training with an injury, the chances are good that you'll eventually break down. You'll end up having many issues, and you're not even sure which one to address first. A nightmare! You must target and treat your longtime problem before it escalates, advances, and synergistically affects other areas of the body.

Once that happens, your options are now limited, and your future is in doubt. If you want to avoid surgical procedures, you must figure out your weaknesses, get a Double TT-e program, and then combine that with full-body training. These steps will give you the best chance to improve your problem and maintain your regular everyday routines.

<u>Step Five: Top 10 Facts that will help you control or reduce Aging Decay!</u>

1. The top disabling aging disorders leading to long-term declines are:
   i. Musculoskeletal
   ii. Mental Disorders
   iii. Sense organ disease (eyes, ears, etc.)
   iv. These progressive disorders often lead to two common fears: losing independence and going to a nursing home. Many of these issues can be reduced or controlled.
2. It appears that having a sense of improving at something or mastering a new skill adds to self-worth, hence, staves off aging. *People that are open to new experiences and have higher levels of learning tend to live longer.* Keep learning!
3. Chronic medical conditions cause half of all deaths worldwide, and nearly four in five Americans live with multiple medical conditions. *The more ailments you have after retirement age, the shorter your life expectancy*, and every additional problem accelerates risk factors and decreases your chances of remaining active. In the US, 60% of people aged 67 and older have multiple chronic diseases.
4. The paradox of aging perception is that aging results in irritable, grumpy, and cranky behavior. The truth is that as we grow older, for the most part, we become happier! Also, astoundingly, perceived health often improves even though objective health is declining. Research shows *that people with derogatory views of aging die earlier than individuals with positive outlooks.* Not a surprise. Stay positive!
5. Getting older is not linked to depression. Emotional and psychological stress lowers your resistance and can accelerate aging dilemmas. Not addressing depression issues can increase the risk for Parkinson's, stroke, pneumonia, and other age-related syndromes.
6. Older people who join a group activity almost always stay in better health, use less medication, have fewer falls, are less lonely, and have a better outlook on life. Extensive research confirms that *social interaction and group networks are viable components of individuals who live long lives.* Be a part of something.
7. Even lean individuals should be beware of central obesity (belly/hip fat), which correlates with increased risk factors for disease. Many researchers report that waist size may be the key to life span, not weight. The bottom line is *more muscle, and less fat is integral, even in people with average weight.*

8. Americans spend more money on health care and drugs than any other country globally, but *greater access to medical treatment doesn't necessarily correlate with better health. If you combine having a healthy lifestyle with medical treatment, your odds of controlling progressive deterioration improve significantly.*

9. Older adults who continue working tend to be much healthier across the board in total body fitness and health outcomes. Workers in the most physically demanding jobs had the lowest risk of bad health. *If you retire, have a plan to do something, not necessarily paid work but something that keeps you involved and motivated.* I rarely agree with Madonna, but I do concur with the motto, "I'll rest when I'm dead." As Newton described, "objects at rest tend to stay at rest, objects in motion tend to stay in motion." Simple brilliance... Keep rolling!

10. Exercise is critical in modulating, mollifying, and moderating aging declines. The extensive literature documenting the negative consequences of inactivity is undeniable and conclusive. Here are just a few of the thousands of facts from authors and researchers in the field of aging factors.

    a. Running five to ten minutes a day can help extend your life.
    b. High levels of physical activity increase the likelihood of surviving an extra ten years free from chronic diseases.
    c. Adults who do 45 minutes a week of moderate activity were 80% more likely to improve or sustain physical function and gait speed for at least two years.
    d. Older adults walking 6000 to 8000 steps a day decrease their chance of dying of heart disease and stroke by 50 to 65%.
    e. Exercise cuts the risk for chronic disease and is also an effective treatment.

In Summary

This chapter outlines ways to modulate and reduce aging factors that result in functional decline and gradual deterioration of your physical function. Our primary objective is to alert individuals that aging can be manageable, barring a catastrophic event. And in many cases, aging declines can be rehabilitated and restored, resulting in a better lifestyle for an extended period. Hopefully, everyone now appreciates that aging is absolute, but deterioration and decline are not determined and are often person specific.

Our central primary concept is establishing a productive, active lifestyle that promotes lifelong participation in physical, mental, and socially rewarding programs. Without a lifetime commitment to a productive lifestyle, all the succeeding guidelines introduced in this manuscript are incomplete and doomed to fail. Lifestyle choices are the integral component necessary to achieve a Super-Aging existence, and you can't build a sound body without this rock-solid foundation.

Countless research articles now document that exercising, a proper diet, staying lean, and not having any addictions effectively maintain long-term health and active lifestyles. The long-term effects of aging declines can be regulated with full-body training and adherence to general fitness. Remember, the goal is to reduce bodily tissue and skills deficits and simultaneously preserve function.

Everyone will have times in their lives when injuries or disease cause significant tissue loss and related skills issues. If you learn to analyze your inherent weaknesses, you may avert other associated problems. Our concept is always to maintain weak areas to preclude long-term collateral issues and growing disabilities. Double TT-e programs focus on stabilizing long-term issues, avoiding significant procedures, and preserving your standard of living.

Our top 10 facts are for your edification. Knowing and understanding the red flags in life can help avoid potential aging declines. How you handle musculoskeletal problems, sense order dysfunctions, and mental disorders can affect your long-term well-being. Try to stay positive, keep learning, be involved in group interactions, and effectively manage periods of depression. Be conscious of the negative consequence of central obesity. Understand that severe medical intervention needs to be followed by short and long-term restoration of function combined with an ongoing commitment to a healthy and active lifestyle. Lastly, adding exercise to your life is critical to anyone who wants to continue participating in an activity and remain independent.

Memorize that aging is all about consistent, progressive, and incremental losses to your vitality. This chapter outlines how Super-Agers maintain body integrity by utilizing active lifestyles. They significantly reduce negative aging decays by incorporating general fitness routines and programs into their lives. They restore aging losses due to injury, disease, or other associated problems and procedures using rehabilitation and ongoing restorative exercise.

Bear in mind that a secret is commonly well known but seldom discussed. This valuable secret needs to be addressed. Aging declines can be manageable if you establish a healthy, resilient, and therapeutic approach to living! A long productive, and functional life span is possible if you make a dedicated commitment to yourself.

Our primary secret is presented using this bedrock model for lifelong adaptations. Maintaining, reducing, restoring, rehabilitating, and repeating for life is our sequential position for preserving a Super-Aging existence for life.

CHAPTER 9: The Importance of an Active Life: Aging Pearls!

Having an active life is an indispensable, vitally important component for maintaining independence. If your goal is to stay relatively free from chronic problems and growing disabilities, always participate, and remain involved in your self-rewarding hobbies and interests. We understand that exercise and sports aren't for everyone, but leading an interactive lifestyle is about as therapeutic as it gets. Remember, being functional includes physical, mental, social, and even spiritual endeavors.

We fully endorse but caution everyone out there who is fully committed, devoted, and spirited about their extracurricular activities. There is no question about the benefits, but some awareness of the pitfalls is advised. This book is all about leading an interactive, up and running, eventful, unchanged, everyday life (barring catastrophe) forever. Sounds simple right?

Living an active life for life is by no means easy; in fact, it's the exception versus the rule. Our average life span is approximately Seventy-Seven for men and Eighty for women in this country. The problem with that statistic is that the length of time spent active and healthy is grossly different for the overall population. Regretfully, the regular person will spend the last ten to twelve years of their later life inactive and in poor health. In contrast, Super-Agers maintain their traditional everyday routine throughout their living years.

These robust seniors have aged, but they're still doing everything they once did; life has not changed much for them. Normalcy for life may sound trivial, but for the elderly, it's an impressive job well done. This accomplishment is incredibly uncommon and reserved for only the best of the best, the Super-Agers.

Why Being Active Is So Important for Everyone

- Activity keeps you socially connected
- Allows you to nurture higher levels of fitness and health
- Controls balance issues, which decreases falls
- Counters depression
- Decreases mental health issues
- Lessens age-related decline of the immune system

- Reduces substance misuse and abuse issues

And best of all, new data shows that physical activity increases the likelihood of surviving or escaping chronic diseases, impairments, and disability for an extra seven to ten years. Unbelievable but true!

Light Activity Is Good but More Aggressive, High-Intensity Movement May Be Better

I know we have primarily lumped all recreational hobbies together, making it seem like they are all equally important for your well-being. That's not 100% true. Please don't misunderstand; unequivocally, we believe that all activity is good, but some physical pursuits involving more movement, including high-intensity cardio, can be better for you in the long run. Let's explain.

New research confirms that high-intensity exercise can enormously benefit the aging population. However, defining high intensity is exceptionally challenging, knowing that some older individuals could injure themselves doing these workouts, maybe even in a way that would necessitate medical care and long-term recovery. So how do you know how much exercise is enough and how much is too much? A profound dilemma! We discuss this premise later in this chapter.

To the Competitive Aging Person, Proceed with Caution

There are examples of aging athletes who experience catastrophic problems resulting in life-changing situations. Sports like skiing, bike riding or racing, marathoning, high-level racquet sports, and even boating and swimming can be menacing in certain conditions. Every person should know that anything is possible, so we suggest you remain consistent and beware of extreme challenges. You need to prepare for aggressive situations thoroughly. Always be aware that the older you get, the higher the risk for injury, disease, and possible emergencies, so tread carefully.

With that being said, let's not compare competitive athletes with lifetime exercisers and people who participate in recreational, fitness, and wellness-based activities. The opposite is true here; there's minimal risk in controlled exercise, and increasing your stamina has high rewards. There is a tremendous benefit for consistent, well-trained people who work diligently at their chosen pursuits. They feel better, look better, and are happier. They can participate in life's many indulgences (food, drink, events, sports, vacations, etc.) because of improved metabolism, better vibrancy, energy, and love of life.

Controlled high-intensity exercise is now documented as broadly beneficial for the aging population. The only thing I can say about pushing the limit too hard is to be careful, be smart, know your limitations, and realize it's not fun being injured.

To the naysayers, who continue to say that healthy, fit, and active people are at greater risk for injury and disease, this notion is simply outdated and erroneous. The benefits of movement, activity, and exercise are now bona fide, conclusive, and indisputable. I sincerely hope that all medical personnel will someday unify and help promote the tremendous benefits derived from an active lifestyle.

What Are the Steps to Take to Remain Active for Life?

1. Design a weekly, monthly, yearly routine, modify as needed, and do it religiously.
2. Establish, sustain, and nurture an active network of people. It is invaluable to have partners that push and encourage each other to continue your chosen sport, hobby, or pastime. A little lite-hardy competition among friends is generally entertaining and motivating, and nothing is more fun than playful bragging rights amongst friends or partners.
3. Sign up for activities, classes, sports, events, tournaments, or other extracurricular things to motivate yourself. If you can't or don't want to get out, set up home programs that you find stimulating and rewarding.
4. Never stop moving for any reason. Even during injury, disease, recovery, or tough times, try to get up and get around.
5. Do weight-bearing and movement activities whenever possible but be aware that strategic brain training games like bridge, chess, pinocle, or other thinking games also count! You're never too old to participate in something.

Whether you're checkmating, trumping, striving for a personal best running, walking, practicing your golf swing, bowling, or playing a racquet sport, always continue to progress, achieve, and improve at something, forever. Make each succeeding year a better year. If you can't reach a higher goal, adjust your goals and move forward from there.

What Are the Pitfalls, and How Do You Get by Them?

1. The main two reasons for stopping activity are illness and injury. Don't let one problem end your active life! Suppose you suffer a long-term breakdown (a few weeks, months, or more), plan on doing adequate rehabilitation before resuming activity.

2. Adapt to life-changing, life-altering situations. Marriage, retirement, job changes, moving, and having or raising children are all major life stressors. Find a new short-term routine. Then once settled in, reestablish activity networks.

3. De-conditioning and weight gain are an invitation to diminished activity, physical losses, and emerging problems. Therefore, staying as active as possible during off-times, vacations, and unexpected downtime is imperative.

4. Don't start a new physical endeavor over and above your current fitness level. Frustration is common, and injuries can be consequential if not adequately trained.

5. Playing through significant ongoing soreness can be hazardous to your health. The general rule of thumb is if pain continues for more than 2-3 days post-activity, it may be time for a professional evaluation.

6. Apathy and burnout are common in aging populations. However, if you maintain a network of friends, who are also committed to that same activity, chances are you'll participate because of social interaction and camaraderie. If one pursuit gets repetitive or tiresome, grab a friend or partner and try something new.

7. If you stop improving or get worse at whatever your chosen activity is, you'll eventually lose interest. So, keep striving to at least maintain, and better yet, improve your skill. And yes, you can improve some skills regardless of age.

8. Do it for fitness, do it for health, do for friendship, do for fun, do it for all the above, and chances are you'll continue.

<u>Aging Pearls</u>

1. Weight-bearing coupled with movement is life's elixir. Aging pathologies and degenerative changes are intimately tied to reduced motion and minimal weight-bearing activity. *Resistance is not your enemy but your friend, and it is the ultimate tool for continued growth.*

2. Maintain spinal integrity. Back injuries are the number one injury globally, and these are often complex problems with no simple answer. Pelvic tilts, bridging, hip and trunk motions, hip flexor, rotator, and IT band stretching are just a few examples. If in doubt, find a good trainer or physical therapist and have them set you up with a program.

3. Don't let your body fold up. Typically, aging results in the lack of extension in numerous joints. Beware of joints that don't straighten or are partially flexed or rotated. These destructive deformational changes (twisted, rounded, bent over), if not addressed, may become permanent.

4. Maintaining a regular walking pattern is crucial if you want to remain active. Restoring gait is almost always possible, barring significant pathology.

5. Understand the principle of active rest. Active rest means that you're also maintaining your general health and fitness whenever recovering from injury or illness as well as addressing other individual problems. You may have to rest the injured area but find ways to maintain other body parts and systems.

6. Don't lose buttock or lower extremity strength. Exercises like straight leg raising, mini squats, and lunges are simple and easy. Get a program and do it 3-5 times a week.

7. Foot deformities can result in total body deficits. In addition, foot pathology and rigid joints (ankle, foot, toes) are some of the leading causes of dysfunctional gait, radiating soreness, and growing weight-bearing issues. Catch these problems early before they become disabling.

8. Chronic inflammations are prevalent in older populations. If you have daily long-term swelling anywhere in your body, find out why. Whether it's due to poor circulation or specific to a joint, this fluid retention will break you down quickly if left unchecked.

9. Bladder and urinary stress are way too common. The elderly population should do pelvic floor exercises (Kegel's) routinely.

10. Activity delays disease and is an effective treatment for a disability. Contrary to common misconceptions, activity decreases long-term musculoskeletal problems and arthritis.

That brings us to a common question that many people ask. What type of activity is best? Let's discuss the new idea of high-intensity versus low-level training.

A relatively new concept in the aging population is that high-intensity training extends life spans and improves the quality of life. Let's review a fascinating study done by Dorthe Stenswold and colleagues. This five-year study examines the effect of exercise training on all-cause mortality in older adults, and it's called the 'Generation 100' study. She says:

"First of all, I have to say that exercise, in general, seems to be good for the health of the elderly. Our study results show that on top of that, training regularly at high intensity has an extra positive effect."

We cautiously agree regarding high-intensity exercise but remember this is extremely person-dependent! Our recommendations are to always stick to consistent routines with short intervals to increase the intensity, as tolerated. Consistent training with gradual progression is practical and reasonable based on your fitness level. Work hard but always work smart. If you're not at an advanced level, marginally trained, or generally unfit, utilize professional assistance.

Aging pearls represents an accumulation of decades of working with and observing typical progressive issues that are predictable and consistent in the aging population. Our opinion is you should never let old age sneak up on you. Many of these long-term changes don't necessarily have to happen. Losing your ability to get around, becoming a crooked person, sagging body parts, frequent soreness, chronic inflammation, and recurrent medical issues are common but not necessarily inevitable. Our message is that you can reduce many of these derogatory changes, enabling you to lead a more productive and meaningful life.

Conclusions:

Staying active for life is no longer overly optimistic, pie in the sky notion from unrealistic aging deniers. The average lifespan in the early 1900s was around fifty years old. Only amazing prognosticators could have foreseen the average lifespan rising to approximately eighty years old and often extending well into the nineties, even hundreds, in 2021.

The problem is that those numbers are somewhat misleading in modern-day society. Our lifespans have lengthened, but our years lived having good health and being ambulatory and self-sufficient are decreasing.

So, what do we do about it? First, let us at least agree that everyone deserves to live their lives with dignity and be able to take care of themselves for their entire life, or at least most of their lives, whenever possible.

A simple social science theory proposed by Robert James Havighurst epitomizes the Super Aging philosophy and is titled the "Activity Theory." It states that older adults are happiest when they stay active, involved, and maintain social interaction; it's that simple.

The reward comes with that exhilarating feeling we all get after accomplishing a goal, learning something new, advancing a skill, finishing a project, or simply maintaining your chosen hobby, activity, or sport. On top of all of that, there's little doubt that you'll be happier, healthier, more physically fit, as well as psychologically and mentally more astute.

The magic of movement is real. Active and rigorous people understand and experience stress relief, euphoria, and a naturally occurring hormone high. You can't get that from a pill!

For those who are passionate about living an active life, you must always, always, always work relentlessly at preserving that lifestyle. Don't count on chance. Don't wait until something happens that changes your life forever. Don't wait until it's too late to adapt and adjust.

Maintaining an active lifestyle translates into extended years of being fulfilled, connected, and in good health. An engaging lifestyle may not always be possible, but the goal is simply to work diligently and enjoy something. These interactions are great for your self-worth and well-being. And finally, the most crucial objective is to always take care of yourself for as long as possible. Maybe in advanced aging (80-90+), leisure time may mean short walks, card playing, shopping, dancing, stretching, or other lower-level pastimes. It doesn't matter what you choose to do if you're still moving, participating, and staying active.

Our aging pearls are nothing more than a reflection of what typically happens in the last quarter of life. Understanding these changes can help you reduce or control these typical growing issues. Super-Agers have earned their moniker by being lifetime achievers. This chapter provided quick tips on achieving that desirable goal that almost everyone wants and desires, being a part of something and the ultimate gift,

Independence for Life!

CHAPTER 10: Discussion and Conclusions

Discussion

Our primary objective in writing this book was to educate individuals about what aging is, how it progresses, what problems it causes, and ways to control long-term changes. Our simple algorithm for aging is to maintain, reduce, restore vital tissue, physical skills, internal capacities, and associated functions. This formula provides a template for aging gracefully. If you then add the ability to identify, treat, and rehabilitate individual weaknesses to pre-disorder status, you now have a working plan to address aging changes.

We explain that Super-Agers maintain healthy and productive lifestyles, have higher cognitive abilities, efficiently absorb oxygen, and continue aggressive physical and mental activities. Best of all, they don't have any significant chronic problems throughout life. These prolific agers are not from a distant planet endowed with incredible powers; they're ordinary people who understand the sacred principles of preserving function and the magic of motion.

In Chapter One, we ask how old are you and are you aging normally? Our aging test examines what abilities you have lost over time. After completing the exam, you should evaluate how, or to what degree, aging has affected you. Invariably, if you can control these losses and preserve your skills, you can ultimately sustain vitality and stay more efficient and operational longer!

Unfortunately, maintaining these living skills can become more problematic because sooner or later, you'll experience a simultaneous health issue, injury, or disease. One of our earlier questions to explore was, when does aging occur? Here's one probable answer? When these dual threats happen, beware; these compounding precipitators frequently accelerate aging if not handled correctly.

The immeasurable possibilities include a traumatic incident, an insidious ache or pain, something internal, a threatening digestive or bowel occurrence, or possibly some new, uncommon, abnormal symptom. Astute observers have learned and now understand that many modern-day problems don't just randomly happen; they incubate over time? Aging factors are relentless, and everyone will experience ongoing issues that can percolate into life-altering situations. This conclusion leads us to recommend that all individuals develop and incorporate a lifetime plan or philosophy to deal with these incidences, like FIGHT for your active life. We will discuss this later in this section.

Here are our favorite aging theories and what we feel they represent. Wear and tear, telomeres, internal clock, and free radicals' concepts. These formulations forecast aging changes over time and conclude that everyone will experience variable degrees of decay and deterioration guaranteed, eventually leading to life-changing situations and eventual death. Still, our premise is that some of these changes can be forestalled, impeded, and somewhat manageable resulting in a better quality of life. Let's explain.

A central theme of this book is to understand that bodily loss due to disease, injury, and degeneration are a certainty, but regaining function is not. Incomplete rehabilitation is often the cause of long-term physical problems leading to chronic conditions. Our philosophy is never to accept partial restorative care.

The recovery process isn't complete following severe medical conditions until you return to pre-injury, pre-disease status. We certainly understand that this may not always be possible with certain people and older groups with advanced issues, but we must strive to meet that goal whenever possible.

Be aware that the aging population, especially seniors, is not always advised to initiate rehabilitation, and some folks are denied treatment. Also, when physical medicine is approved, it usually is limited, not allowing full recovery. Why this is happening is up for debate but be aware that Medicare capitated (highest level of reimbursement) coverage in 2021at $2100 for outpatient therapy services.

Complete restorative care for severe incidents is unlikely to be completed under those guidelines, and continuing services would create a financial burden to the patient. Seeking alternative care is an option but would probably still be cost-prohibitive.

Frequently, older patients who receive this abbreviated physical treatment are told that their therapy has been completed and they've reached an appropriate level of progress. Is that true, or is it more likely that your insurance reimbursement is complete? To be fair, many physicians do try to appeal some of these decisions, when appropriate, with minimal success. Unfortunately, these truncated treatments rarely result in the successful restoration of function, and these incomplete treatments often result in long-term problems. We hope that these older patients can complete their care within the boundaries of their insurance coverage in the future.

Think about it! Are Americans overall leading lives conducive to health maintenance and disease control, or are they just reacting to medical needs as necessary? Too many Americans, particularly seniors, have been seduced into a world of premature treatment, especially prescription drug use touted as prohibitive care. It doesn't sound like preemptive care; it sounds more like ongoing, forever, drug-centric treatment. We understand completely that some of these medications are necessary, but are all these copious drug-related treatments helping?

If these inhibitory pharmaceutical treatments are working, why does this country spend more on medicine than any other country globally, yet we are not in the top 30 for healthy or total lifespan?

Seniors' top three most common disabling conditions are musculoskeletal problems, mental disorders, and sensory dysfunctions. Regretfully, these problems are at best minimally covered by insurance carriers, including Medicare. Why, and what can we do about it? We have seen some movement by insurance companies to address common aging predicaments; hopefully, these expansions will continue to progress.

Also, is it time to universally promote necessary coverage for the physical evaluation of musculoskeletal problems? A one-time assessment would be cost-effective and likely improve the lives of many seniors struggling with looming disabilities. Initiating in-home rehabilitation focused on maintaining activities of daily living and conjointly promoting accessory programs and productive living standards for the aging population could help millions of seniors have a better quality of life at a minimal cost.

We must respond to those individuals who genuinely believe that the current population is more active, fit, and healthier than the previous few generations. How often have you heard someone say 70 is the new 60? Or that we are so much more active than our parents or grandparents were? I'm not sure why people think that way but let's review.

The straightforward facts are:

a. The past few generations were substantially more physically active in all life parameters, making the need for added movement, exercise, and other leisure-time activities less crucial.
b. Technology has consistently improved many components in our lives but also significantly weakened our bodies.

We are blessed with less arduous living, and everything is automated. Even physical labor jobs are machine-based and minimally physical. We don't even turn on our lights anymore; we just ask Alexa to do it.

The truth is that contemporary lifestyles are slowly eroding our bodies resulting in compromised function. Talk about a pandemic; look around! We are experiencing an unprecedented rise in unhealthy, unfit, overweight, and inactive people, causing acceleration and proliferation of disease and disability conditions. An old catchphrase epitomizes this preponderance of a mostly high standard of living: "Hard times create strong people; strong people create good times. Good times create weak people; weak people create hard times". Be on your guard!

We're living longer, but our later years are tenuous at best. Our late-stage quality of life is in jeopardy if we don't change our behavior. We sincerely hope that everyone will make that all-important decision to alter their destiny by adding movement, activity, exercise, and overall physicality back into their life.

Conclusions

Primary risk factors include inactivity, unhealthy weight, addictive behavior, poor diets, hypertension, type two diabetes, and stress. These disease-causing players predominantly happen over extended periods. These developmental conditions are not spontaneous; they grow, spread, and advance over years and decades.

We can preempt premature aging and threatening afflictions by promoting healthy living through movement, activity, exercise, diet, and therapeutic programs.

Remember this quote from the WHO, "There is no such thing as a typical 80-year-old person." This statement challenges the stereotypical notion that everyone will suffer catastrophic issues. As you probably know, there are immense differences in older individuals' health and activity status. A significant degree of dedication and choice is involved in aging gracefully and maintaining normalcy.

Will you choose to look at aging as a time for growing experience, knowledge, skill, and most importantly, wisdom, leading to high expectations and a quality standard of living? Or will you be a doomsayer with the pessimistic thought that you will experience decay, deterioration, weakness, leading to disease and eventual tragic death?

Another vital concept to conceptualize is to become a Super-Ager; you must constantly be adaptive and enthusiastic. Everyone's goal in life should be to always remain as normal as possible, with a steadfast and confident mentality. In that case, you'll have the best chance of overcoming most issues and simultaneously continue to grow in some way.

There are many possible pitfalls that the aging population may incur. Everyone will experience nonspecific and uncertain illnesses, injuries, and breakdowns, with no exceptions. Every bodily system will be affected, making aging the most prominent known risk factor to injury and disease.

Why are Super-Agers able to survive, escape, and delay these aging issues until much later in their lives? One of the primary reasons is they don't fall prey to any long-term chronic conditions because they fully recover from significant problems.

Super-Agers have involved lifestyles, continually challenge themselves, and are social. They regularly indulge in vigorous but disciplined movement, treat themselves yet control food choices, drink limited amounts of alcohol and caffeinated beverages, take exotic vacations, etc. They are overwhelmingly happy, resilient, and constantly engaged in something. They prove our thesis: Activity for life improves living! Also, remember these behaviors are consistent and not excessive.

Another invaluable hypothesis to grasp, endorse, and believe in is that the number one cause of physical breakdown today is previous injury and lack of complete rehabilitation from that issue. If ignored, you're just another problem waiting to happen, leading to the discontinuation of valuable recreation and the initiation of chronic treatment.

What do we need to understand about aging truths, falsehoods, myths, and mysteries? A central truism is that everyone will experience many physical issues, and it's essential to realize that most of these problems are treatable and controllable throughout life. Unfortunately, too many people don't grasp or simply disregard this absolute truism; *age does not usually restrict recovery.* Remember, remarkable progress can be made, even with the very old.

Prevalent falsehoods and myths are somewhat frightening, disturbing, and in many ways downright scary. Some of these myths are that you're destined to have dementia, osteoporosis, arthritis, lose your libido, lose your drive, lose your energy, and always be sick. On top of that, people say you'll also be poor, lonely, frail, incontinent, in pain, and lose all your teeth. Although there is some truth in all the above scenarios, most of these sensationalized later life issues don't generally happen and are not the norm. Do not accept these false perceptions as reality.

The most significant and prominent myth that everyone needs to understand, and rebuke is that physical activity is harmful to your health. This egregious fallacy is by far the worst of all falsehoods and myths. Not only is your involvement in activity not dangerous, but it's incredibly therapeutic and the fundamental component for total body health and fitness.

Exploring mysteries are fascinating and could be covered in an entirely separate book. Philosophical discussions regarding what affects aging, ways to maintain our vitality, and, in turn, slow the aging process are widespread and highly provocative. Can we eliminate major diseases, extend life, and even become immortal? These fascinating topics may be explored in future books. In the meantime, we will leave it up to all of you aspiring Plato's to decide what the future holds.

We also address the five most common causes of disability and early mortality, and those conditions are heart disease, cancer, respiratory problems, stroke, and accidents. A key finding is that a high percentage of these syndromes can be impeded, limited, successfully treated, or curtailed.

Risk factors like addictions, high blood pressure, high sugar, high cholesterol, high body fat equal HIGH RISK! A significant percentage of these primary disease-causing factors are reducible. In contrast, good fitness, good health, a good diet, good muscle tone, normal body fat, and being active result in LOW RISK! You do, almost always, have a wide degree of choice.

There are five other absolutes in long-lived lives besides death and taxes. You will experience different degrees of bone loss, muscle loss, postural changes, orthopedic issues, and arthritis, guaranteed. With maybe the exception of some acute orthopedic problems, all these issues are primarily long-term and progressive. There are only two ways to deal with these dilemmas, control the losses and, in turn, reduce long-term problems or regretfully succumb to them.

A vital feature in our Super-Aging paradigm is the F.I.G.H.T for your active life acronym. Faith and fortitude, illness and injury, genes and growth, health and habits, training and transitions are the cornerstones of these guidelines for living. Without these integral components, navigating life's relentless journey can be daunting. Everyone should develop their own specific version of this comprehensive working philosophy that works for them.

You must have faith and fortitude and always recover fully from illness and injury. Through activity and exercise, you can continue promoting bodily growth. Knowing your heredity and history should help you recognize weaknesses that may affect your lifelong pursuit to age gracefully.

The best defense against breakdowns is good health produced by good habits. You should continuously work on a lifetime plan to maintain your strengths and reduce weaknesses. Keep going consistently at your own pace and adapt, adjust, and transition when needed. Life is not a sprint; it's a marathon.

Super-Aging quotes this classic inspirational passage from the movie Independence Day for elder motivational purposes. Some backstory: Humans were being threatened with extinction from an alien invasion and had to fight for their lives. The theme is in some ways analogous to aging individuals fighting for their life when threatened with a notable injury, disease, isolation, loneliness, and depression. The result is the possible loss of independence. I've revised the quote below:

"Senior individuals must forget their petty differences and unite behind a common cause [aging concerns]. We must fight for our freedom, fight for our right to live, to exist. We will not go quietly into the night; we will not vanish without a fight. We're going to live on; we're going to survive!" Today we stand united and declare Seniors Independence Day!

HOORA., HOORA! Now, don't forget to include this all-important axiom from Chapter One, "Don't keep me alive by keeping me from living," then ask yourself, how hard will you fight for your freedom, for your everyday life, and for your right to live it?

There is a tremendous difference between the total length of life (years lived) versus the number spent participating and involved. The average active and healthy life span for women is 69.5 years, and for men, it's only 66.8.

That means that older women, living the average lifespan, are compromised for the last 12 years of life, and men have reduced capacities for the last decade. Living somewhat disabled for 10-12 years, in our opinion, is tragic. Super-Aging believes that you can narrow that gap considerably and enjoy a more satisfying and productive lifestyle longer.

The idiom, *you're only as strong as your weakest link*, was a precipitator of our new concept called Therapeutic Targeted Exercise (Double TT-e). These specific plans are designed to help injured individuals recognize their primary weakness(es), knowing that if these deficits are left unchecked, other issues will frequently escalate into a host of related problems. Isn't it finally time to stop saying to yourself, *I'm falling apart*, and do something about it?

This book was written as a health and fitness manual with a therapeutic theme. Being involved in physical health for most of my life made me realize that physical medicine is underutilized, especially for the aging population.

Super-Aging does not doubt that every senior (no exceptions) will have musculoskeletal problems that trained physical medicine specialists could help alleviate. The fact that we have one or every three seniors fall every year, resulting in thousands of deaths, should be a wake-up call to anyone concerned with looming aging issues.

Currently, life spans are plateauing, and worse yet, our late-stage quality of life is also diminishing. We believe combining medical advancements with a commitment to healthy lifestyles, total body exercise, and physical restorative exercise medicine is an excellent way to address, control, and reduce aging changes; we hope you agree.

This book would not be complete without reviewing what the top Super-Aging Secrets are:

1. You can control or reduce aging changes by consciously preserving vital tissue, physical skills, internal capacities, and associated function.
2. Always maintain skills, reduce tissue losses, and restore function. These lifestyle adaptations will produce healthy and robust bodies and reduce progressive disease-causing factors.
3. Super-Agers should aggressively work at full recovery, therefore eliminating chronic problems.
4. Not only do you not wear down due to activity and exercise, but it is also highly beneficial and therapeutic.
5. Be aware that only 15% of seniors aged 85 need dependent care. The point is that you can take care of yourself if you maintain your daily abilities and overall health.
6. The great majority of seniors are not dying from acute or chronic infections. Degenerative diseases are our elder's biggest threat, and the secret is that many are reducible and controllable.
7. If you can eliminate early risk factors, you can limit developmental late-stage conditions, lowering the incidence of severe diseases.
8. You are never too old to rehabilitate, and even the most elderly can frequently restore lost muscle, bone, and function.

In closing, let's reiterate these well-known core concepts of healthy living: don't smoke, avoid addictions, stay lean, exercise daily, maintain a healthy diet, and control stress.

And for those people who want to create the best chance of being Super-Agers, here are some valuable pearls and suggestions to live by:

- Never stop moving, interacting, staying involved, and always strive to learn new things.
- Always maintain an upright neutral posture.
- Do daily weight-bearing, range of motion, and flexibility training.
- Always work on spinal and pelvic movement.
- Maintain hip and lower extremity strength.
- Work on gait and balance every day.
- Don't let your body fold in. Always work on having end-range extension in all joints.
- Do everything possible to complete the recovery process and get as close to normal after significant injury or disease.

We leave you with this question to ponder: *You only have one life to live; what type of life will you choose?*

- Will you just take your chances?
- Will you employ the aging advice given throughout this book to repress growing decay, deterioration, and disease?
- Will you utilize knowledge and wisdom to attenuate weakness and disability?

Choosing to focus on the optimistic side of aging will enhance your life as you grow older. Wouldn't everyone like to be remembered as a structured, self-sufficient supportive person who loved life, lived life, and touched many people positively along the way? Now that's a memorable journey.

Super-Aging believes that everyone needs to find their well-defined pathway to a more meaningful, active, and fulfilling life for life. That's the goal!

Further Reading:

1. Teemu Niiranen, MD., Hypertension, online. Research Fellow, Boston University School of Medicine, Framingham Heart Study; Bryon Lee, M.D., professor of medicine, director electrophysiology laboratories, and clinics, University of California, San Francisco; May 30, 2017.

2. The US. Department of Health and Human Services. The Health Consequences of Smoking-50 years of Progress: A Report of the Surgeon General, Atlanta. Office on Smoking and Health, 2014, accessed 2018, Feb.22.

3. Farhad Islam; M.D., PhD., Morbidity, and Mortality weekly report, online; strategic director cancer surveillance research. American Cancer Society; October 3, 2017, media briefing; US. Center For Disease Control and Prevention. Morbidity and Mortality weekly report, online.

4. News Review published September 5, 2017, in Cancer Prevention Research: An international team of researchers looked at data from 20 existing studies:

5. NIH Cancer Institute report published on February 10, 2020. Physical Activity Fact Sheet.

6. NIH Press Release, May 16, 2016. Increased Physical Activity Associated with Lower Risk of 13 Types of Cancer.

7. New England Journal of Medicine 2017: 376;178-181, 10-year outcomes in Localized Prostate Cancer.

8. American Cancer Society report on 5-year survival rate for localized cancer, published February 2, 2021.

9. American Academy of Dermatology website updated 6/1/2021.

10. Health Day, 6/29/2017: Melanoma Results Can Differ, Worrying Patients.

11. Brooke Nickel, The Conversation, Medical Press: Is it time to remove the cancer label from low-risk conditions? August 13, 2018.

12. Len Horovitz, MD., pulmonary specialist, Theo Vos, professor at the University of Washington, Seattle. The Lancet Respiratory Medicine: Lennox Hill Hospital, New York City, August 16, 2017. Nearly 4 million Die Each Year from Asthma or COPD. The Lancet Respiratory Medicine.

13. Medline Plus: Respiratory Disease Death Rates Have Soared; September 29, 2017.

14. Medline Plus: Uptick in the US. Stroke Deaths Sets of Alarms: CDC., July 18, 2016.

15. Medline Plus: 9 out of 10 Strokes Could Be Prevented, Study Finds; July 18, 2016.

16. NCHS Pressroom, July 14, 2021. Drug Overdose Deaths in the US. Up 30 % in 2020.

17. Transformation Treatment Centers (2021website): How many people die from prescription drugs?

18. Center For Ethics: New Prescription Drugs, A Major Health Risk, 6,27/2014.

19. John Hopkins University: 250,000 deaths per year due to medical error in the US. This report was published on May 3, 2017, in the British Medical Journal.

20. CDC Press Release May 1, 2014; Up to 40% of Annual Deaths from each of five leading US. Causes are preventable.

21. CDC Report May 15, 2018; 31% falls-related deaths increase to 29,668.

22. National Safety Council concludes that poisoning deaths rise to 65,773 in 2021 press report.

23. National Safety Council show as many as 42,060 people are estimated to have died in motor vehicle accidents in 2020 report online.

24. Cruz, A.J. et al. Age and Aging, Oct. 2014: One in three adults 50+ suffer progressive muscle loss, research shows.

25. Needham Dale, M.D. A longer stay in hospital ICU has a lasting impact on quality of life, 4/2/2014.

26. Lohman Timothy PhD., Going Scott PhD.: The Best Exercise Program for Osteoporosis Prevention, Fourth Edition-Jan 1, 2017.

27. NIH: Osteoporosis and Related Bone Diseases, National Resource Center; Osteoporosis Overview; last reviewed 2019-10.

28. BMJ 2019; 364;1902, How much medicine is too much.

29. Jarvinen Teppo, Ph.D.; Hip Fractures Prevention Drugs Cause More Harm Than Good; Health Line, October 16, 2019, by Cathy Cassata.

30. The Good Body; Back Pain Statistics; December 11, 2020.

31. Freburger Janet K, Pt, Ph.D. et al.: The Rising Prevalence of Chronic Low Back Pain; Arch Intern Med, 2009, February 9; 169 (3) 251-258.

32.   JAMA Surg. Published online February 28, 2018, DOI 10. 1001/JAMA Surg. 2017-6231
33.   Hawker Gillian Dr. Not all patients benefit from hip or knee replacement; Journal Arthritis and Rheumatism, April 4, 2013.
34.   CDC website; Arthritis: Current 2021 online.
35.   Arthritis Foundation: Arthritis by the Numbers, 2019; V3; 4100.17.10445.
36.   Single Care website; Arthritis Statistics, 2021.

ABOUT THE AUTHOR

Angelo Moca is a lifelong professional exercise, fitness, and rehabilitation advocate with a master's degree in sports medicine and a bachelor's in education. Angelo has spent his entire life working with all age groups and populations. His experience includes being the Head Athletic Trainer for the Chicago Sting professional soccer franchise, the Senior athletic trainer for Olympia Fields Medical Center, and the physical medicine and rehabilitation specialist for the Center for Sports Orthopedics. He is also the founder and President of Back in the Game, a therapeutic exercise company that works with the older population to help mature individuals maintain active lifestyles.

Angelo has spent a lifetime developing his expertise in rehabilitation and training. His new passion is working with aging individuals who want to preserve their ability to stay active for life. Angelo's extensive, wide-ranging amount of experience is revealed in Super-Aging Secrets. His message is *you don't have to live your life in fear, thinking you'll eventually become disabled. Living a productive and meaningful life, for life, is possible if you learn how aging enthusiasts beat the clock.*

Go to Super-Aging.org for more information.

Made in the USA
Columbia, SC
25 March 2022

58092662R00083